Kid-friendly adventures

WAIKATO, BAY OF PLENTY & CENTRAL PLATEAU

THE ULTIMATE FAMILY GUIDEBOOK

Ceana Priest

HAPPY ADVENTURES!

From bubbling mud pools and volcanoes to historic mining tunnels and forests saved by eco-warriors, the Waikato, Bay of Plenty and Central Plateau regions are the perfect stomping ground for intrepid explorers. We have loved exploring all the areas, and include our favourite adventures in this guidebook.

After Finn was born, I struggled to find trails suitable for buggies and his little legs — memorably ending up knee-deep in a lake on a 'buggy-friendly' trail! So I started Outdoor Kid and began sharing our walks and bike rides. I wanted to help families find adventures that would instil a love of the outdoors into their mini-explorers — and not have to head home after unexpectedly meeting stairs while out with the buggy or bike.

So, happy adventuring, and we hope you'll discover the joys of climbing volcanoes, peering into ancient gorges, hot-pool wallowing and learning about New Zealand's remarkable native flora and fauna along the way.

Ceana and Finn x

Outdoor Kid | Ceana Priest

E. hello@outdoorkid.co.nz

W. outdoorkid.co.nz

OUR TOP SPOTS

BEFORE YOU GO

PLANNING

Make sure your trip suits the abilities of ALL family members. Take a map, or download one to your phone. Share your plans with others, and tell them when you expect to be home.

WEATHER

Always check weather conditions (metservice.com) before heading outdoors on an adventure. Things can change fast.

BE PREPARED

Make sure you have enough food and drink to match the length and conditions of your walk.

GEAR TO TAKE

BASIC FIRST-AID KIT
For cuts, bruises and bites

INSECT REPELLENT
For pesky biters

RAIN AND WIND JACKET
For all conditions

WATER BOTTLES
Filled up

MOBILE PHONE
Fully charged

LOTS OF SNACKS
AKA bribes!

SUNGLASSES AND HATS
Summer is hot hot!

EXTRA WARM LAYERS
Just in case

IN AN EMERGENCY CALL 111

WHAT TO WEAR

STAY COOL IN SUMMER AND TOASTY WARM IN WINTER

WARM OUTER LAYER

No matter what the weather conditions are when you start your adventure, always take a warm outer layer like a jumper or a polar fleece top. Even on hot days, it can be much cooler in the forest. So, you may quickly chill when you stop to play beside a stream or for a picnic.

HAT AND SUNGLASSES

Protect yourself from the sun's UV rays. Levels are especially high between September and April. Even when it's cold and cloudy, remember to slip, slop, slap and wrap. A thermal beanie when the temperature cools is vital to keep your head warm.

BASE LAYER

For adventures during cold weather, your base layer should fit snugly to your body to trap in body heat. Try and avoid cotton, which takes AGES to dry if it gets wet. Synthetic or merino materials perform much better as a base layer.

In summer, wear something loose-fitting with room for a cool breeze to sneak in.

INSIDE YOUR BAG

Slip in a waterproof and windproof jacket just in case. And it doubles as something to sit on when it's time for lunch. Don't forget to pack plenty of snacks and water, too.

SHOES

Hiking boots with grippy tread are great if you're exploring in the mountains. Sneakers are perfectly fine for adventures closer to home. Save an old pair, so it doesn't matter if they get muddy.

JUST IN CASE!

What could you spot with a pair of binoculars? Perhaps a native kererū/wood pigeon crash-landing through the trees? Take a photo! Or, grab your pencil and sketchbook and sit quietly in the forest, drawing native plants. Up for an adventure? Grab the torch and go glowworm hunting.

OUR FAVOURITE

TOP SPOTS TO EXPLORE

WATERFALLS

Head to Rotorua to see folks plunge off the world's largest commercially rafted waterfall near **OKERE FALLS** (left, p125).

Walk past mammoth moss-covered boulders before climbing to the top of the 153-metre-high **WAIRERE FALLS** (right, p74).

VOLCANOES

Stroll along the flanks of Mount Doom on New Zealand's best one-day walk, the **TONGARIRO CROSSING** (right, p166), and marvel at the alpine scenery and pretty emerald lakes.

Peer into the steaming bowels of an ancient volcano surrounded by towering barren orange and red cliffs from **MAUNGA KĀKARAMEA SUMMIT TRACK** (p128) near Rotorua.

GEOTHERMAL ACTION

Discover spluttering mud and crystal-clear thermal waters at **TOKAANU THERMAL WALK** (right, p153) near the shoreline of Lake Taupō.

Wallow in a steaming natural hot pool created by the mingling waters of the thermal **OTUMUHEKE STREAM** (p138) and the chilly Waikato River near Taupō.

BEACHES

Poke around tall volcanic rock columns and small, sunbeam-lit caverns beneath a headland at **CAVE BAY** (above, p93) before visiting postcard-worthy **OROKAWA BAY** (p92) near Waihi Beach.

Avoid the masses at the secluded **ŌTARAWAIRERE BEACH** (p114), hidden behind a headland from Ōhope Beach and accessible only on foot or by kayak.

HISTORICAL GEMS

The **PUNAROMIA ROCK ART** (p126) waka motifs were submerged for nearly two decades after the Tarawera eruption but are now visible.

How were the mysteriously rectangular rock blocks of the **KAIMANAWA WALL** (right, p145) created? Drive through stunning beech forest to find out.

MORE ADVENTURES ONLINE AT:
OUTDOORKID.CO.NZ

WAIRĒINGA/BRIDAL VEIL FALLS | NEAR RAGLAN

EXPLORE THE MIGHTY

WAIKATO

Wedged between the windswept black sands of the wild Tasman Sea coast and soaring eastern mountain ranges, this adventure-laden region offers nature-lovers waterfalls tumbling off ancient lava flows, glittering underground glowworm grottos and wetlands for endangered native birds.

HIGHLIGHTS

JOURNEY DEEP INTO A MOUNTAIN ALONG AN ABANDONED RAILWAY TUNNEL

Walk through a historic rail tunnel stretching for more than a kilometre, surrounded by rocky landscapes where miners braved treacherous conditions in the 1800s, searching for gold (p82).

BOARDWALKS CLING TO CLIFF FACES AND GLOOMY CAVERNS TEMPT BRAVE EXPLORERS

For free highlights of the rugged Waitomo limestone landscape, explore Ruakuri Walk along a narrow gorge draped in native ferns and dewy moss, with glowworms creating a magical after-dusk light show (p66).

LEGEND TELLS OF A MYSTICAL BUSH-CLAD AMPHITHEATRE, HOME TO MIST-DWELLING FAIRIES

Admire the 55-metre-high Wairēinga/ Bridal Veil Falls near Raglan from accessible lookouts before trekking to its misty base, surrounded by cliffs exposing raw, ancient lava flows (p57).

TĪKAPA MOANA/FIRTH OF THAMES

PŪKOROKORO BIRD HIDE TRACK

Become an enthusiastic bird-twitcher for a few hours and scout for thousands of wading birds, including flocks of the remarkable kuaka/bar-tailed godwits returning from their Arctic tundra breeding grounds each year.

The internationally recognised wetland at Pūkorokoro/Miranda covers 8500 hectares along the Firth of Thames. And although its unique geology is impressive, the main drawcard are the diverse flocks of avian residents who call this wetland home, sometimes only temporarily. Make the most of this adventure by visiting the Pūkorokoro Miranda Shorebird Centre on East Coast Road to hire binoculars or a telescope. From the centre, walk to the three viewing hides (allow 1 hour return) or drive 2 kilometres south to Robert Findlay Wildlife Reserve for a shorter adventure. At the reserve, follow the 400-metre-long Bird Hide Track to the hides to avidly birdwatch. Two hours on either side of high tide are best for bird viewing and, during summer, volunteer shore guides are available at the hides to help identify birds lurking in the shallows.

LIME WORKS FACTORY

The landscape includes a series of shell ridges formed over 4000 years, creating the Miranda-Kaiaua Chenier Plain. Remnants from a shell-crushing factory that operated until the mid-1950s producing lime are beside the car park. Tugboats and barges transported lime to local farmers around the Firth of Thames, who used the powder to 'sweeten' their land.

PŪKOROKORO MIRANDA SHOREBIRD CENTRE

Chat with the friendly volunteers from Pūkorokoro Miranda Naturalists' Trust about identifying birds and the team's impressive conservation efforts making a difference globally. Open every day from 9am to 5pm except Christmas Day. Entry to the centre is free, although donations support the trust's work raising awareness of coastal ecology and helping shorebird research and education. Shop for excellent all-ages books and gifts or stay overnight in the accommodation. Their website has recent bird sightings.

FIND OUT MORE
shorebirds.org.nz

INFORMATION

GRADE: Easy.

ACCESSIBILITY: Well-graded track suitable for buggies and wheelchairs (grab a gate security code from the centre; walkers don't require a code).

TIME: Bird Hide Track, 5 min (400 m) one way. Return from the Shorebird Centre to the hides is 1 hour (4.5 km).

FACILITIES: Toilets at the centre.

LOCATION: The Pūkorokoro Miranda Shorebird Centre is on East Coast Road south of Kaiaua on the Firth of Thames.

DOGS: No dogs.

KUAKA
BAR-TAILED GODWIT

These incredibly plucky birds make the longest non-stop flight of all birds, and, because they don't dive for food, they often fly for more than 11 days on an empty tummy.

Godwits begin arriving at the Firth of Thames in early September after travelling more than 11,500 kilometres from the Arctic regions of Alaska. They are one of 35 species flocking to New Zealand each summer to either fatten up on plentiful food supplies or avoid winter in their chilly frozen homelands.

Some 80,000 godwits arrive each year and can also be spotted elsewhere around the country, including the Manukau Harbour, Farewell Spit and Avon-Heathcote estuary.

In March, godwits leave Pūkorokoro in small flocks after spending the warmer months in New Zealand. Several birds have been resighted more than 28 years after first being banded — now that's a lot of air miles!

MĀORI NAME

Māori named the godwits kuaka. Because of their migratory habits, they were considered a bird of mystery. 'Kua kite te kōhanga kuaka? Who has seen the nest of the kuaka?'

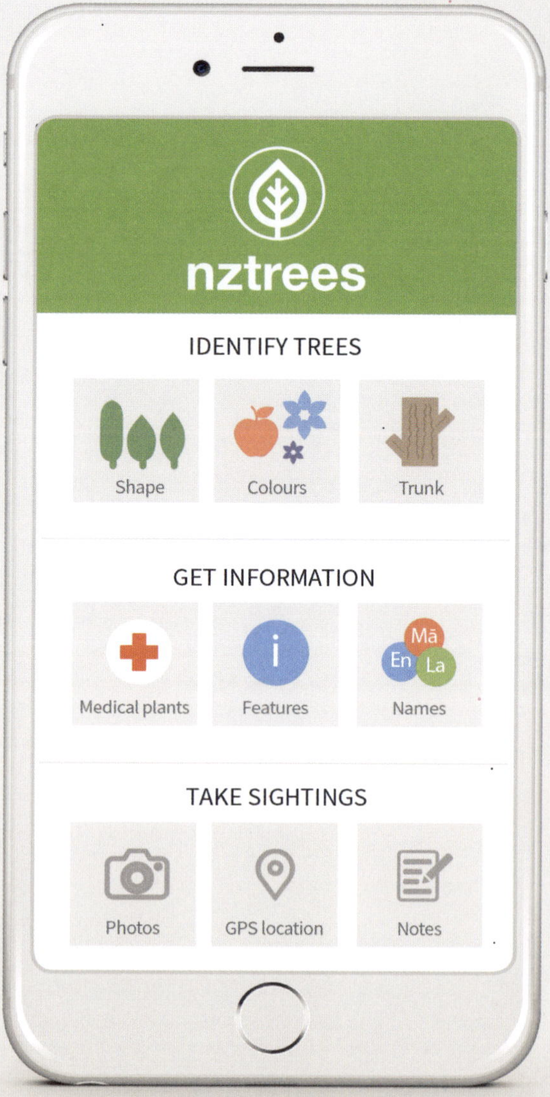

BY THE COAST

SHOREBIRDS AT PŪKOROKORO

How many remarkable birds can you spot on the Firth of Thames's shell banks and tidal flats?

1. POAKA | PIED STILT

These dainty wading birds are widespread at wetlands and coastal areas. They have slender necks and long legs, which help them feed in deep water. They are a self-introduced species and arrived from Australia around 1800. They are notorious tricksters at distracting enemies from their nest and will fake injury or even death.

2. TARĀPUKA | BLACK-BILLED GULL

Although similar-looking to the red-billed gull, the tarāpuka is more slender and has a longer bill. They are quite shy and generally mind their own business. Unfortunately, introduced predators like cats and stoats mean this gull – which is native to New Zealand – has become one of the world's most threatened gull species.

3. TŪTURIWHATU NEW ZEALAND DOTTEREL

These endangered native birds build their nests above the high-tide mark on the beach, which unfortunately is close to where human activity occurs. Their camouflaged nests and eggs can be destroyed by vehicles or horses on the beach. They are monogamous (having only one partner at a time) and can vigorously defend their territory.

4. KŌTUKU-NGUTUPAPA ROYAL SPOONBILL

The first royal spoonbill was recorded in 1861 at Castlepoint on the Wairarapa coast, and the first breeding was recorded in Ōkārito (Westland) in 1949. They often feed in shallow wetlands, alone or in small flocks. Watch as they submerge their bill and sweep it side to side to feed. The adults develop long white plumes on the back of their heads.

5. TŌREA | VARIABLE OYSTERCATCHER

These coastal waders are very protective parents and can aggressively dive-bomb to defend their chicks. They are often spotted busily probing around on beaches and estuaries looking for shellfish. They open mussels and cockles by inserting their bill tip into the shell rim and twisting, or by hammering.

6. KŌTUKU | WHITE HERON

These beautiful birds breed only at Ōkārito Lagoon in Westland, although they are regular visitors to the Firth of Thames. Each year in August, they return south to coincide with the īnanga/whitebait run, which is their primary food while nesting. Elsewhere in New Zealand, they eat frogs, skinks and small fish. The white heron has a population estimated at between 150 and 200 birds.

PORT WAIKATO

PORT WAIKATO SAND DUNES

Clamber to the tops of these vast dunes before gravity takes over and you plunge down the billowing mounds at full speed. Contented, exhausted kids are almost guaranteed on the homeward drive.

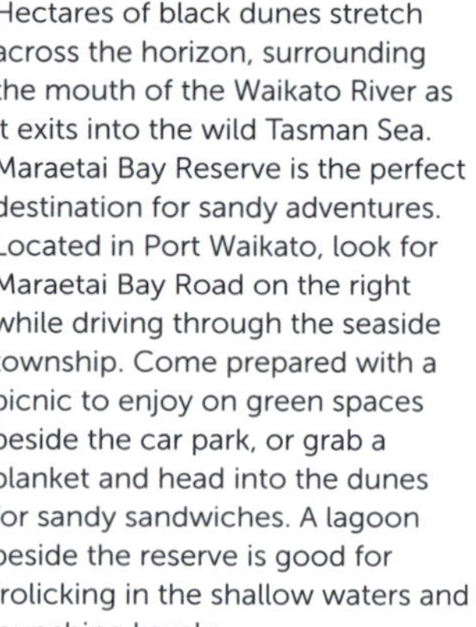

Hectares of black dunes stretch across the horizon, surrounding the mouth of the Waikato River as it exits into the wild Tasman Sea. Maraetai Bay Reserve is the perfect destination for sandy adventures. Located in Port Waikato, look for Maraetai Bay Road on the right while driving through the seaside township. Come prepared with a picnic to enjoy on green spaces beside the car park, or grab a blanket and head into the dunes for sandy sandwiches. A lagoon beside the reserve is good for frolicking in the shallow waters and launching kayaks.

EXTEND THE ADVENTURE

If there are fossil fossickers in the family, continue to Sunset Beach and poke around the cliffs and coastal rocks at the southern end for ancient critter and shell remnants. Alternatively, a stroll along the wind-whipped sands will fill the lungs with salty air. Although the beach is picturesque, it has powerful currents and rips, so swim only when the local Surf Life Saving Club is on patrol.

ĪNANGA | WHITEBAIT

This small native fish, with its silvery belly, is found in coastal rivers, wetlands and lakes throughout New Zealand.

Īnanga migrate downstream between February and May to lay eggs in dense vegetation flooded by spring tides. The eggs are stranded when the water retreats, hatching at the next spring tide before heading out to sea and munching on plankton for six months. During their return, while migrating back up streams, they are called whitebait – the most commonly caught of the six whitebait species found in New Zealand.

INFORMATION

GRADE: Easy.

ACCESSIBILITY: Lots of hot black sand. Shoes are better than flip-flops.

TIME: Allow a couple of hours to explore the dunes, play in the small lagoon and picnic — more for visiting Sunset Beach.

FOOD OUTLETS: A few options, including dairies.

RUBBISH: Bins provided.

GETTING THERE: Head west from Pōkeno through Tuakau. Follow the Tuakau Bridge–Port Waikato Road to Port Waikato.

DOGS: On leads.

FACILITIES: Plenty near the car parks.

IMPORTANT: Don't forget sunscreen and hats.

THIS BEACH HAS STRONG RIPS AND CURRENTS, LARGE WAVES AND DEEP HOLES. THIS BEACH IS PATROLLED ONLY WHEN LIFEGUARDS DISPLAY YELLOW AND RED FLAGS. ALWAYS SWIM BETWEEN THE FLAGS.

FIND OUT MORE
doc.govt.nz

HAVE YOU SEEN AN

ENDANGERED MĀUI DOLPHIN?

Māui are the world's rarest and smallest dolphins and are on the edge of extinction. Only between 48 and 64 dolphins over one year of age are known to exist.

They live on the west coast of the North Island from Maunganui Bluff to Whanganui, and you're most likely to spot them between the Manukau Harbour and Port Waikato. They were once common along the entire west coast of the North Island.

They look the same as Hector's dolphins but are genetically different. Māui used to be known as the North Island Hector's dolphin, but in 2002 were classified as a separate subspecies. They both have a rounded black dorsal fin; all other dolphins have a sickle-shaped fin.

These amazing dolphins are slow to reproduce, with females producing only one calf every two to four years.

Keep an eye out for Māui while you explore the coastline, as they are often spotted in water less than 20 metres deep. They have distinctive grey, white and black markings and a short snout. The males are slightly smaller and lighter than the females, which can grow to 1.7 metres in length and weigh up to 50 kilograms.

SPOTTED A MĀUI DOLPHIN?

Report any Māui dolphin sightings to the Department of Conservation by calling 0800 362 468. If possible, include location, GPS coordinates, number seen, time and date.

ONEWHERO

TE WAI HEKE O MAOA/ VIVIAN FALLS

Despite being a rather sombre landmark in Māori history, this nīkau-shrouded waterfall is also a scenic detour after exploring the rolling dunes of Port Waikato.

In the 1700s, warriors seeking revenge on the powerful chief Tapaue were ordered to lie on jagged rocks beneath the 12-metre-high waterfall. Above, the temporarily dammed river was released, pummelling the warriors below. When none left their positions, their strength was considered a promising sign for the upcoming battle.

Walking from Harker Reserve at the end of Miller Road only takes a few minutes, or 3 kilometres from Onewhero–Tuakau Bridge Road.

INFORMATION: No facilities. Rocks can be extremely slippery.

LOCATION: Harker Reserve at the end of Miller Road, Onewhero.

SH1 HUNTLY

TE IRINGA LAGOON

A meandering path beside the Waikato Expressway (SH1) explores a regenerating scientific reserve where over a million native plants have been grown from locally sourced seeds.

The wide gravel track leads to four impressive waka maumahara/ memorial waka, each representing one of the four winds that blow through the valley. Further along, relics of Rua's Hut, built in 1879, are visible — unfortunately, only chimney remnants and orchard fruit trees remain.

Native shrubs and harakeke/flax line the lagoon's pathway, and giant wizened tree stumps have become mini-ecosystems for little critters — kids can clamber over the large upturned roots. Allow 20 minutes return.

INFORMATION: No facilities.

LOCATION: Accessible southbound only on the Waikato Expressway SH1, Huntly section.

SH1 MERCER

WHANGAMARINO HISTORIC WALK

Perched on a grassy spur overlooking the Waikato and Whangamarino Rivers, Te Teoteo's pā held a desirable vantage point during the Waikato Wars of the 1860s. Its raised location provided vast vistas across the landscape, from where warriors could view enemies preparing for battle. A 30-minute loop climbs several flights of steps to the pā site, before continuing to the nearby British-built Whangamarino Redoubt, from where troops attacked Māori forces at Meremere. After exploring both fortifications, return the same way or follow the old roadway used during the Waikato Wars back to the car park. From the lookout, young train buffs may spy a few engines chugging past on the Main Trunk Line.

INFORMATION: No facilities.

LOCATION: Oram Road is 2 kilometres south of Mercer on SH1. Parking is beside the control gates over Whangamarino River.

TAUPIRI

MOUNT TAUPIRI

Hidden beneath the mountain's lush nīkau-clad flanks lies a well-trodden trail that ascends the southern end of the Taupiri Range, leading to a trig with impressive wrap-around views.

INFORMATION

GRADE: Medium/Hard.

ACCESSIBILITY: Dirt path with steps.

TIME: Allow 2 hours return.

FACILITIES: Toilet at the cemetery.

LOCATION: Parking at the end of Watts Grove off Orini Road, Taupiri.

DOGS: On leads.

This sacred maunga holds an immensely important place in the hearts of Waikato Māori, as it is the resting place not only of revered Māori royal family members but many other prominent tīpuna.

It's also a maunga which doesn't reveal its views easily; this adventure isn't for the faint-hearted. Follow the 4WD track through the cemetery from the car park and pass beneath the archway. The trail climbs steadily — very steadily — for almost 900 metres until it reaches the trig at 288 metres above sea level. Hopefully, a cool breeze here will sweep past the bulbous nīkau palms, supplejack vines and well-nibbled kawakawa leaves to soothe sweaty foreheads.

Near the top, turn left at the unsignposted junction to the trig, surrounded by a small grassy clearing. Rest and refuel, with sweeping views across Huntly and the southern volcanic peaks of Kakepuku (elevation 449 metres), Mount Pirongia (959 metres) and Maungatautari (797 metres) providing an impressive backdrop.

Return the same way or turn left at the junction to follow a slightly overgrown ridgeline winding down to the 4WD track for a five-minute stroll back to the car park. Both options take roughly the same amount of time.

HUNTLY

LAKE HAKANOA

Winding through expanses of swampy wetlands and various themed gardens, an easy, well-maintained path encircles the 52-hectare lake located in the mining township of Huntly. Native harakeke/flax and toetoe line the pathway leading to the Green Cathedral, a tranquil outdoor church popular for weddings.

Nine-year-old Ted Smith planted the majestic oak tree near the edge of the lake in 1923, which still stands today. In the distance, steam from the Huntly Power Station — New Zealand's largest thermal power station — billows into the sky. There's a post-adventure playground and skate park to explore for children with energy left after roaming around the lake.

INFORMATION: Allow 45 min to 2 hours (3.6 km) for the loop. Toilets, picnic tables and playground.

LOCATION: Parking is available at Huntly Domain on Taihua Road, off Park Avenue.

HORSHAM DOWNS

LAKE KAINUI

Snaking alongside the shallow shoreline of a small but picturesque peat lake on the northern outskirts of Hamilton, this easy trail winds through densely clumped stands of trees and past camouflaged maimais — some shabby through to quite impressive.

The well-graded path gives newly minted riders a chance to test their two-wheeled skills, although in mid-winter the path can become softer.

From the car park, choose either direction to explore the lake; both options have westward views of the bush-clad Hakarimata Range and farmland.

INFORMATION: Allow 1 hour (about 3 km) for the loop. Toilet (clockwise from the car park), picnic tables and plenty of parking. Check the gate closure time on arrival. Closed during duck-hunting season (about May and June).

LOCATION: Lake Road, Horsham Downs.

NGĀRUAWĀHIA

KĪNGITANGA HERITAGE TRAIL

Laze on grassy banks at The Point, watching the Waipā and Waikato Rivers converge, before enjoying a leisurely exploration of this riverside township to learn about the history of the area.

There are several starting points, although The Point is near the skate bowl, flying fox and playground. Beside the band rotunda are trail maps and information about the 1860s wharf catering to steamers plying their trade, former pā sites and other historic gems.

Keen to extend your adventure? Bring the bikes and tackle the Te Awa River Ride (p38) south alongside the Waikato River.

INFORMATION: Allow 30 min for the loop.

LOCATION: Lower Waikato Esplanade, Ngāruawāhia.

TAUHEI

PUKEMOKEMOKE BUSH RESERVE

Boardwalks wind up the flanks of Mount Pukemokemoke beneath stands of kauri and past historic Māori sites to a trig surrounded by 360-degree views of the Waikato Basin.

INFORMATION

GRADE: Easy or Medium.

ACCESSIBILITY: Dirt paths, boardwalks and steps to the trig.

TIME: Allow 80 min return for the Bush Loop Track or 5 min one way to the picnic area.

FACILITIES: Toilet near the picnic area.

LOCATION: Tauhei Road, Tauhei.

DOGS: On leads.

A network of trails exploring 40 hectares of lowland forest thriving with kauri, tōtara, mataī and kawakawa lead to a grassy clearing, perfect for summer picnics and year-round adventures. Although extensively logged until the 1950s, this maunga is still forested with kauri and rimu at least 300 years old, because luckily loggers felled only the largest trees, leaving plenty of reasonably sized trees to mature.

Older explorers will quickly tackle the stairs and 400-metre-long boardwalk above fragile kauri tree roots to the lookout 166 metres above sea level. From the car park, the trailhead is opposite the entry bridge. Meandering up the mountain, the trail passes leafy kawakawa trees renowned for their medicinal use. Among the encroaching flora is a historic site used by travelling Māori as a temporary shelter, and deep trenches and food pits are still visible. From the summit, enjoy planning more adventures to Pukemokemoke's sister peaks of Taupiri (p17) and Pirongia (p47).

For a more accessible outing, a spacious grassy area surrounded by forest is 5 minutes from the car park and is perfect for picnics and playing within the forest edge. A kawakawa-lined dirt trail is suitable for buggies after cleaning them at the kauri dieback station.

Friends of Pukemokemoke Bush Reserve have been restoring flora and fauna within the reserve for nearly two decades — donations support their endeavours.

PŌKENO

PŌKENO WATERFALL

Locals descend on this small waterfall when summer arrives to practise impressive manus. Thundering dive-bombs are often heard long before the small waterfall comes into view. It's also the site of a former Māori flour mill — some relics, including the steel and timber waterwheel, can be seen beside the wide, sometimes steep, gravel path.

INFORMATION: Walking only, 5 min to the waterfall. Dogs on leads. Check for submerged dangers before swimming.

LOCATION: Te Ara Aukati Terrace, Pōkeno.

ROTOKAURI

LAKE ROTOKAURI

Stroll to one of the region's largest peat lakes on the northern outskirts of Hamilton. Towering harakeke/flax bushes line a winding boardwalk through regenerating wetland before it emerges near the lakeside. Dangle a line and spend a sunny afternoon fishing or enjoy a snack at the picnic tables. Return the same way or follow the dirt path back to the car park.

INFORMATION: Buggy- and bike-friendly. Allow 45 min to 1 hour for the loop. Dogs on leads.

LOCATION: Parking at the end of Bunyard Road, off Rotokauri Road near Rotokauri School.

HUNTLY

LAKE PUKETIRINI

The lake's former life as an open-cast coal mine is hard to imagine, with grassy landscaped grounds and regenerating native forest now circling the popular swimming and kayaking spot.

INFORMATION: Allow 1 hour to walk around the lake. Dogs on leads. Buggy- and bike-friendly.

LOCATION: Rotowaro Road, Huntly.

TE KŌWHAI

TE OTAMANUI LAGOON

An easy, flat, kōwhai-lined trail leads to a sprawling lagoon where tuna/eel and kākahi/freshwater mussels were once plentiful. An effort is underway to restore the lagoon's ecosystem.

INFORMATION: Allow 1 hour (about 4 km) return. Buggy- and bike-friendly. Dogs on leads.

LOCATION: Parking beside Te Kōwhai Hall on Horotiu Road.

RANGIRIRI

RANGIRIRI PĀ

Explore the fortification remains at the site of one of the fiercest battles of the Waikato Wars. Information signs within the historic reserve share the stories from the engagement.

INFORMATION: Allow 30 min to explore. Walking only. Dogs on leads.

LOCATION: Car park off Te Wharepu Road, Rangiriri.

HAKARIMATA RANGE

KAURI LOOP TRACK

Get close to a huggable 1000-year-old kauri on the Hakarimata Range's northernmost tip, and, if little legs allow, hike to a vantage point with panoramic views of the north Waikato.

INFORMATION

GRADE: Medium or Hard.

ACCESSIBILITY: Well-graded path with steps.

TIME: Allow 40 min to 1 hour return to Kauri Grove. Allow 90 min (3 km) for the entire loop.

FACILITIES: Basic toilet near the car park.

LOCATION: 10 km north of Ngāruawāhia, turn onto Parker Road, off Hakarimata Road. Plenty of parking.

DOGS: No dogs.

Looping beneath dense native forest and past serene kauri groves, the trail leads to a mighty kauri tree, one of the biggest in the Waikato. But explorers must navigate a healthy dose of stairs before reaching the girthy native for a snuggle.

From the car park, several long flights of stairs lead to the trail junction. For a steep, thigh-busting climb to the lookout, continue straight ahead. Or swing right for a sedate stroll along a well-graded trail towards the main attraction, a 1000-year-old kauri tree. This section is suitable for most explorers, although younger children may request a piggyback.

After cuddling the 36-metre-high kauri and viewing the rickers (young kauri) growing nearby, return the same way or continue upwards along more flights of stairs to a vantage point with views of the Waikato River, Lake Waikare and Lake Puketirini (p20).

From the lookout, it's a quick descent back to the car park.

However, a grove of native trees beside the trail junction has identification labels to read — a good spot for a breather.

HAKARIMATA RANGE

HAKARIMATA RAIL TRAIL

During the warmer months, this sun-speckled wallowing hole at the base of a small waterfall is a crowd-pleaser for all ages.

INFORMATION

GRADE: Easy.

ACCESSIBILITY: Well-graded dirt paths. Steps to the waterfall.

TIME: Allow 30 min (1.7 km) one way walking to the waterfall. 10 min biking one way to the junction.

FACILITIES: Basic toilet near the picnic area.

LOCATION: About 2 km south of Ngāruawāhia on Waingaro Road.

DOGS: No dogs.

Tracing the route of the former Ngāruawāhia/Glen Massey railway, this mainly flat, well-graded trail is ideal for young bikers graduating from concrete to dirt paths. Following alongside Firewood Creek past regenerating wetlands, the biking trail is graded easiest (Grade 1) — nothing strenuous. Or, explore by foot for a leisurely family stroll.

After the picnic area, return the same way. Or, with more time, don't miss the Cascade Waterfall flowing down exposed rocks into a shallow pool shaded by native forest. Unfortunately, there's no biking on the final 200-metre-long waterfall path, so if arriving on two wheels, secure bikes to the rack at the trail junction before visiting the waterfall.

On warm days, the pebble beach and shallow stream beside the waterfall are accessible for young kids to dip their toes, while older kids can clamber over the rocks and plunge into the chilly swimming hole.

GLEN MASSEY RAILWAY

Further west on the overgrown railway route is the wreckage of a runaway coal train that crashed in 1933 after leaving the Glen Massey shunting yard. Driver William McLean remained with the train and its six carriages to sound the whistle and alert people on the track. Unfortunately, the train derailed at Windy Creek, where the heroic driver died. The wreckage is not accessible from the trail.

HAKARIMATA RANGE

HAKARIMATA GLOW-WORMS

For a quick dusk adventure, follow the shallow Mangarata Stream as it flows beneath a dark forest canopy to a small waterfall spilling over an old dam. Climb steadily on the well-maintained trail beside the stream, passing swathes of parataniwha (p68) and navigating several flights of steps.

Damp forest banks surround the waterfall, cloaked with thousands of twinkly glowworms luring critters to their sticky, luminous strands.

Only 15 minutes from the car park, the grotto is perfect for an after-dinner outing. Return the same way. Bring a torch to look for tuna/eels slithering downstream in the dark stream.

INFORMATION: Walking only. Allow 30 min (about 2 km) return — more for ogling the glowworms. No dogs. Dirt paths and steps. Toilet beside the car park.

LOCATION: Parking on Brownlee Avenue, Ngāruawāhia.

HAKARIMATA RANGE

HAKARIMATA STEPS

This gut-busting stairway is popular with fitness fanatics who enjoy brutal climbs and post-workout wobbly legs.

Follow the well-graded trail beside Mangarata Stream to the base of the stairs. While clambering up the 1349 steps, folks on their way down often provide cheerful encouragement.

At the viewing tower 374 metres above sea level, there are views of Ngāruawāhia, Hamilton and across to the Kaimai Range. A challenging adventure suitable for older kids.

INFORMATION: Walking only. Allow 2 hours return. No dogs. Dirt paths and wooden steps. Toilet beside the car park.

LOCATION: Parking on Brownlee Avenue, Ngāruawāhia.

HAKARIMATA RANGE

WATERWORKS WALK

A historic 750,000-litre reservoir in the foothills of the Hakarimata Range provides a short forest adventure filled with critters and fluttering pīwakawaka/fantails. Luckily it also avoids the nearby strenuous Hakarimata Steps.

From Brownlee Avenue, follow the Mangarata Stream and continue straight at the Hakarimata Steps junction. Steps wind up beside the small spillway leading to the water's edge and a broad gravel area. Bring insect repellent if planning to linger, as there are some active biters. Built in 1922, the reservoir once supplied water to Ngāruawāhia.

INFORMATION: Walking only. Allow 1 hour (about 2 km) return. No dogs. Dirt paths and steps. Toilet beside the car park.

LOCATION: Parking on Brownlee Avenue, Ngāruawāhia.

FIND OUT MORE
resi.org.nz

image © Gary Clare

RIVERLEA

HAMMOND PARK

Wedged between a forested cliff face and the Waikato River surging past is a long, meandering boardwalk that kids will love tearing along.

Home to the tiny pekapeka-tou-roa/long-tailed bat, this native forest remnant overlooking the Waikato River can easily be explored within half an hour.

It feels a little prehistoric, with trees looming over the boardwalk before views broaden near the curved boardwalk bridge. Viewing platforms along the way provide glimpses of the river flowing towards Port Waikato.

When settlers arrived in the Waikato, the river's banks proved too challenging to clear, ultimately saving this thriving forest remnant rich with flora and fauna. It is also a critical wildlife corridor for tūī and kererū to swoop into from neighbouring forested areas in Pirongia and Maungākawa to feed. The site has a long history from when Ngāti Wairere first established a nearby pā.

Beside the Malcolm Street entry are a small playground and a sandy riverside beach for picnicking and letting the dogs paddle. There are other access points, but Malcolm Street is the easiest for an out-and-back adventure.

Or bike to Tamahere Village on the Te Awa River Ride (p38). Bikes must be walked on the boardwalk.

INFORMATION

GRADE: Easy.

ACCESSIBILITY: Concrete paths and boardwalks.

TIME: Allow 30 min return.

FACILITIES: No toilets.

LOCATION: Plenty of parking on Malcolm Street, Riverlea.

DOGS: On leads.

PEKAPEKA-TOU-ROA LONG-TAILED BAT

Hammond Park is home to these little mammals, which weigh only 8 to 14 grams and have a wingspan of about 250 millimetres. However, habitat loss and feral cats and rats are reducing population numbers throughout the country. They munch on flying insects such as moths, midges and mosquitoes, and become less active during the chillier months, with some even entering a semi-hibernation state to conserve energy. Bats roost upside down in small cavities in large old canopy trees such as rimu, pūriri, tōtara and pukatea.

image © Gerald Kelly

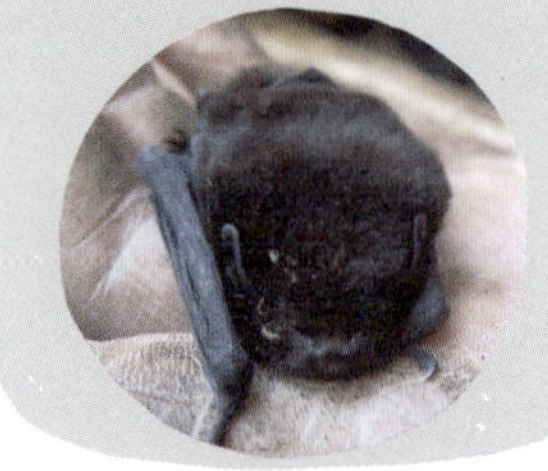

SH23 WEST HAMILTON

TAITUA ARBORETUM

Sheltering wide, easy trails are towering collections of trees hand-picked from around the world, making this woodland on Hamilton's outskirts a peaceful, well-visited destination.

INFORMATION

GRADE: Easy.

ACCESSIBILITY: Well-graded dirt paths.

TIME: Allow 1 hour for a brisk loop walk.

FACILITIES: Toilets at the car park.

LOCATION: Follow SH23 towards Raglan, turn off at Howden Road and then Taitua Road. Open from 8am until 30 minutes before sunset.

DOGS: On leads.

Despite its popularity, the often crowded car park — and its collection of resident chickens — doesn't mean paths full of jostling people. Instead, somehow everyone disappears into the 20-hectare park, providing peaceful family strolling.

The main trail loops past grazing cattle to woodland forests and even a zen bamboo enclave with ponds teeming with frogs. As autumn approaches, vibrant displays of colourful leaves appear in the forest canopy.

This remarkable park is the result of former landowners John and Bunny Mortimer's passion for growing native and exotic specimens. The couple began planting trees and shrubs in the 1970s with no grand plan in mind, but over time their efforts blossomed into a full-fledged arboretum that was eventually gifted to Hamilton City Council in 1997.

Bring a picnic lunch to enjoy under one of the wooden shelters peppered throughout the park, or stay hydrated with fluoride-free water at the car park.

FAIRY HOUSES

Keep an eye out for whimsical fairy homes tucked into tree roots. And there's often a stash of 'Tron Rocks' to discover, or bring some to re-home.

TILLS LOOKOUT

Extend the adventure by another 1 hour (return) by starting at Tills Lookout on Melva Street in Dinsdale. Enjoy 360-degree views across the city towards the foothills of Mount Pirongia while walking to the arboretum. Or just visit Tills Lookout for a quick 15-minute dose of greenery.

HAMILTON EAST

HAMILTON GARDENS

Take 'flight' on a steam-punk airship or carefully tiptoe past mysterious — and slightly ominous — topiary organisms with long, quivering tendrils.

Allow half a day to explore this international-award-winning garden. Probably more. It is the region's most visited tourist attraction, and rightly so. Amble through far-flung countries and cultures — in the heart of the city. Hamilton Gardens is definitely not a traditional botanical garden.

The garden had unlikely beginnings; flanked by the Waikato River, the site was originally a barren dumping ground for the city's waste, with seagulls squawking overhead. It wasn't until the 1980s that the rubbish dump began to be transformed into a magical landscape telling the story of gardens through time. This unique concept was the brainchild of former director Dr Peter Sergel, who garnered community support for the project and oversaw thousands of hours of volunteer labour. Displays of some of Dr Sergel's earliest design sketches are in the information centre — marvel at how accurately each garden reflects his original concepts.

Kids can disappear through mysterious passages, hunt for hidden doors and be unleashed on the playground — especially the earthworm poo slide! New gardens open regularly.

There is a café overlooking Turtle Lake with plenty of options to refuel the family, and toilets near the information centre. During summer weekends and public holidays the enclosed gardens are extremely busy between 11am and 3pm — visit earlier or later to avoid the crowds. The enclosed themed gardens are open daily from 9am to 5pm (last entry at 4.30pm), while the wider parkland areas are open 24/7. Free drinking water stations are available.

The enclosed gardens are currently free, although an entry fee is expected to be introduced in late 2023/early 2024.

All images on p26–27 © Hamilton City Council

FIND OUT MORE
hamiltongardens.co.nz

INFORMATION

GRADE: Easy.

ACCESSIBILITY: Well-graded concrete and dirt paths. Some gardens have steps.

TIME: Allow at least a couple of hours to explore the themed gardens.

FACILITIES: Café, playground, baby-changing room, accessible toilets, gift shop and information centre.

LOCATION: Parking is available through Gates 1 and 2 off Cobham Drive.

DOGS: No dogs are allowed in the themed gardens, but are allowed on leads elsewhere.

GARDEN HIGHLIGHTS

While traditional botanical gardens focus on plant collections, these collections explore the history, context and meaning of gardens while giving an insight into different civilisations. It's like visiting a museum with carefully curated exhibitions reflecting garden history. Some highlights include:

PARADISE COLLECTION

Indian Char Bagh Garden
Italian Renaissance Garden
Japanese Garden of Contemplation
Chinese Scholars' Garden

PRODUCTIVE COLLECTION

Te Parapara Garden
Ancient Egyptian Garden
Sustainable Backyard
Kitchen Garden

FANTASY GARDEN

Surrealist Garden
Picturesque Garden
Concept Garden
Mansfield Garden
Tropical Garden

ROGERS ROSE GARDEN

Visit when the flowers bloom in November for a sensory overload of wonderfully whiffy fragrant roses.

DESTINATION PLAYGROUND

Find the secret garden of Abdul Kabul, and let the kids clamber over the timber treehouse and tire themselves out on the swings and slides.

BAVERSTOCK

WAIWHAKAREKE NATURAL HERITAGE PARK

This wetland on the city fringes beside Hamilton Zoo is becoming a regenerating native forest filled with noisy birdlife — vastly different from its beginnings as barren farmland.

Over nearly two decades, more than 350,000 trees and shrubs planted by volunteers and community organisations have created a retreat for kōtare/sacred kingfisher, ruru/morepork and matuku moana/white-faced heron. And, hidden among the rushes could be the world's thinnest caterpillar, Fred the Thread!

The Northern Loop leads up to the car park opposite Hamilton Zoo through well-established planting. The Southern Loop takes in the lake's main highlights, including viewing platforms above the lake. Various land types are signposted within the 60-hectare park, showing diverse ecosystems such as the lake edge and basin to ridge and hill slopes.

A repurposed barn provides shelter during soggy weather and has information on the wetland and the working farm surrounding it. Hamilton City Council took ownership of the park in 1975.

WAIKATO PEAT LAKES

Hiding beneath the surfaces of the region's 31 peat lakes are hardy critters, including whirligig beetles, seed shrimps and even freshwater jellyfish, while reclusive native birds stalk through the shallows eyeing them up. Peat lakes take thousands of years to form, the tannin-stained water coming from high levels of dissolved organic matter leaching from the peat (formed from the build-up of partially rotted plant material). This process creates an acidic environment which some plants and animals have evolved to cope with. However, any changes to this water balance by human activity can threaten species which have adapted over time.

Take a stroll around other peat lakes, including Lake Kainui (p18) and Lake Rotopiko (p43).

FIND OUT MORE
wetlandtrust.org.nz

FRED THE THREAD

Discovered hiding in giant cane rush stems growing in Waikato peat bogs, this little critter's claim to fame is that it might be the world's thinnest caterpillar.

Dr Corinne Watts of Manaaki Whenua — Landcare Research was investigating how to restore peat bogs after mining when she spied some unusual markings on the cane rush and found a tiny, thin, orange caterpillar. No one was quite sure what it was, so, along with her colleague Dr Robert Hoare, she gathered more cane rush stems and waited for the little insect to appear. What emerged was a beautiful moth less than half a centimetre long, with a wingspan of only 12 millimetres. It was nicknamed 'Fred the Thread' after its caterpillar, and is a previously unknown moth genus.

Its scientific name is *Houdinia flexilissima,* which relates to Harry Houdini, the famous escape artist, and how flexible Fred is, using its flip-top head to navigate through the slender cane rush. Although Fred is safe at Waiwhakareke Natural Heritage Park and Lake Rotopiko, elsewhere the caterpillar's natural habitat is at risk from being drained for pasture, fertiliser input and fire.

Fred image © B. Rhode, Manaaki Whenua — Landcare Research

INFORMATION

GRADE: Easy.

ACCESSIBILITY: Well-graded paths and boardwalks.

TIME: Allow 1 hour return.

FACILITIES: Toilets near the shelter.

LOCATION: Parking opposite Hamilton Zoo on Brymer Road or near the southern entrance on Baverstock Road.

DOGS: No dogs.

TEMPLE VIEW

LEGACY PARK

Boardwalks zigzag through shady stands of trees leading to wooden shelters with views of a rippling lagoon and mini fountains.

This excellent short adventure for kids can be wrapped up in under 30 minutes, unless they want to burn off more energy on the all-ages hillside playground with its forts, swing bridges and winding slides.

Learn about the early Mormon missionaries from the nearby Hamilton New Zealand Temple inside the shelters.

INFORMATION: Remember to slip, slop, slap and wrap, as there's no shade at the playground. Toilets and a drinking fountain are available. Dogs on leads. Walking and buggies only on the boardwalks, no bikes.

LOCATION: Foster Road, Temple View.

CLAUDELANDS

TE PAPANUI/JUBILEE PARK

Snaking past lofty kahikatea trees, this inner-city forest filled with winding boardwalks can easily be explored within 15 minutes. But despite being a short adventure, urban life feels miles away while walking beneath the dense canopy filled with plenty of chirping birds. Navigate trees poking through the boardwalk, lined with ferns and tangled supplejack vines.

Before modern settlement, vast semi-swamp lowland forests covered the area. Today, only this 5-hectare remnant remains, filled with tawa, māhoe and buttressed pukatea trees, along with at least 40 native land snail species that have been discovered here.

INFORMATION: Allow 15 to 20 min to complete the loop. Easy grade on wide, flat boardwalks.

LOCATION: Entrances at Claudelands Park and on Brooklyn and Boundary Roads.

NEWSTEAD

NEWSTEAD WALKWAY

Murky swamps, towering eucalyptus trees and forest shelters will delight little explorers. The farm-flanked entrance off Vaile Road is the quickest route to the clearing and small boardwalk to spy tuna/eels in the dark, muddy waters. Some inexpensive meat might tempt the slippery carnivorous natives from the shallows. Bring insect repellent if hanging out near the swamp. A notable eucalyptus tree on the northern edge of the clearing once measured 72 metres tall, but in 1968, when the storm that caused the *Wahine* disaster swept across the nation, the tree lost more than 3 metres off its crown. Until then, it was considered one of the nation's tallest trees.

INFORMATION: Allow 1 hour return. The entry and exit points of the clearing are diagonally opposite each other – sometimes a little tricky to see. Suitable for buggies and bikes. Dogs on leads.

LOCATION: The trail connects Morrinsville Road and Vaile Road.

PUKETE

PUKETE FARM MTB PARK

Fun, twisty single-track trails suitable for all skill levels wind beneath towering trees and across shrubby landscapes on the northern fringes of Hamilton.

Once a working farm and commercial sand quarry, this sprawling public park underwent a significant makeover in the late 1990s when a team of enthusiastic bikers from the Hamilton MTB Club set about clearing the gorse-ridden landscape and removing the rusty remains of dumped cars.

They have created a popular destination providing about 11 kilometres of winding, sometimes challenging trails catering to young bikers up to more seasoned riders. Navigate through stands of mature trees across bridges, stream crossings and culverts. Free-draining sandy soils provide great year-round riding.

WHERE TO START?

From the main entrance on Māui Street, bike down into the 'sandbox' and follow the markers towards Pukete Road, where it levels out before looping back to the start.

Quick access to easy, flat sections of the park is available from Pukete Road.

HAMILTON MTB CLUB

Catering to all abilities, this friendly club promotes a fun social environment while focusing on getting riders out on the trails. Summer and winter racing series help hone skills for beginners through to elites. Annual individual and family memberships are available.

FIND OUT MORE
hamiltonmtb.org.nz

INFORMATION

FACILITIES: Toilets and water at the Māui Street entrance.

TRAIL GRADES: Easy (Grade 2) and intermediate (Grade 3).

OPENING HOURS: Riders can access the park 24 hours.

ENTRANCE FEE: Free, although donating to Hamilton MTB Club helps maintain the tracks.

ARE E-BIKES ALLOWED? Yes.

ARE DOGS ALLOWED? Dogs are allowed on leads within the park but must remain 10 metres away from bike trails.

IS RUNNING OR WALKING ALLOWED? Not on the trails.

LOCATION: Roadside parking is beside the main entrance at 66 Māui Street in Te Rapa. More sedate trails are accessible opposite the Te Awa River Trail car park near the water-treatment plant on Pukete Road.

LET LOOSE ON THE
CITY'S PLAYGROUNDS

HAMILTON EAST
PARANA PARK

This kōwhai-themed garden is a magnet for kids cooling off and splashing in the shallow paddling pools in summer. Swoosh down the slide, get soaked by 300 jets squirting from a giant kōwhai seed or play on the small playground.

LOCATION: Parking on Memorial Drive, Hamilton East.

image © Teamturf

CENTRAL CITY
HAMILTON LAKE DOMAIN

Everything families need for a lakeside outing: a large climbing fort, an old-school slide to test kids' nerves, a fenced toddler area, cascading water-play area with an Archimedes' screw and accessible swings. Bonus: there's an ice cream kiosk and café nearby for an after-play treat.

LOCATION: Rotoroa Drive, off Ruakiwi Road, Central City.

HAMILTON EAST
HAMILTON GARDENS PLAYGROUND

Kids can warble tunes or frolic on the open-air stage before scaling the wooden fort, exploring the nature-themed playground and finding the secret garden — a playground for all ages.

LOCATION: Gate 2, Cobham Drive, Hamilton East.

image © Hamilton City Council

HAMILTON EAST
MAGICAL BRIDGE PLAYGROUND

A fully fenced, inclusive playground designed for adventurers of all ages and abilities. Surrounded by grassy mounds and kahikatea trees, this fun, shaded, colourful play space will open in late 2023.

LOCATION: Heaphy Terrace, Claudelands.

image © Magical Bridge Trust

ROTOTUNA
TAUHARA PARK

There's plenty to keep older kids entertained — from tube slides, swings and a basketball half-court to a zippy flying fox, or climb to the top of the spider's webs for a bird's-eye view of the sports fields and gully. Bring the family pooch to the nearby off-lead dog exercise area.

LOCATION: Callum Brae Drive, Rototuna.

NAWTON
DOMINION PARK

Slides plunge from the enormous wooden fort dominating this fun, sprawling ecological-themed park. And it's not only for older kids — youngsters can dip their toes in the water-play areas dotted around the park or build sand creations.

LOCATION: Dominion Road, Nawton.

FOREST LAKE
MINOGUE PARK

A popular playground beside Lake Rotokaeo with bumpy scooter tracks and oodles of fun, kid-friendly activities: slides, tunnels, trampolines, a flying fox and an interactive wooden play feature for summer splashing. Bring bikes to the nearby BMX track.

LOCATION: Moore Street, Forest Lake.

FLAGSTAFF
HARE PUKE PARK

This colourful eel-themed park was voted one of New Zealand's best playgrounds and straddles different play areas: a winding bike track for BMX and scooter riders, a play area for little kids, sand play, and a climbing frame with a flexible, bouncy slide.

LOCATION: Hare Puke Drive, Flagstaff.

HAMILTON LAKE
INNES COMMON

Up the ante at this lakeside urban parkour and outdoor gym where there's enough to challenge the most active of kids. Dual slacklines provide an opportunity for some friendly family competition. Then grab a breather on seats overlooking Lake Rotoroa.

LOCATION: Lake Domain Drive, Hamilton Lake.

HILLCREST
HILLCREST PUMP TRACK

This hub is popular with two-wheeled devotees for its long, looping pump track with smooth berms and humps, while younger kids can tootle around the bike-skills area. All ages will enjoy the playground with its basketball court, hamster wheels, swings and exercise equipment.

LOCATION: Cambridge Road, Hillcrest.

WETLANDS

FISH, BIRDS AND CRITTERS

These often elusive creatures thrive in Waikato wetlands. Good luck spotting a pūweto!

1. TAUHOU SILVEREYE/WAX-EYE

These friendly birds arrived by themselves in the 1800s and live throughout New Zealand in wetlands, forests and urban backyards. They are slightly smaller than a sparrow and are not considered endangered. They munch on insects, fruit and nectar. Tauhou means 'stranger' or, more literally, 'new arrival'.

2. PĀTEKE | BROWN TEAL

These endangered waterfowl were once common throughout the country, but numbers have declined since the 1880s. With population estimates below 2500, they are scarce and at risk of extinction due to predators and habitat loss. Males have shiny heads.

3. BLACK MUDFISH

These fish can survive out of water sometimes for months when their wetland dries out in summer. They burrow under tree roots or into the mud. They are found nowhere else in the world, which makes them pretty cool. They lower their metabolism into 'hibernation' mode until water returns, then they swim away!

image © Waikato Regional Council.

4. PŪWETO | SPOTLESS CRAKE

These mysterious birds are about half the size of a common blackbird and are so secretive they are hardly ever seen. They are reasonably common in the upper North Island, however, including at Lake Rotopiko near Ōhaupō. They build nests under the shelter of mānuka/New Zealand tea tree and forage for food near shallow water under cover of dense raupō/bulrush or harakeke/flax. They quickly hide when disturbed.

5. WEWEIA | NEW ZEALAND DABCHICKS

Māori named this bird after the sound of its occasional shrill call 'weeee-ee'. They anchor their nests to aquatic vegetation, which means the nests can be swamped by small rises in water level, especially boat wash. They are great divers (up to 4 metres) and can hold their breath for about 40 seconds.

6. NURSERY WEB SPIDER

This spider's webs are not for catching prey. Instead, they are little nurseries for young spiders. The female builds the nest when the young are about to emerge from the egg sac she carries during summer. The young nursery web spiders remain safe inside for about a week until they throw out a small thread to be caught by the wind – which is their way of 'leaving home'!

HAMILTON EAST

AJ SEELEY GULLY

Brimming with native and exotic trees, this ecological gem was once barren, unproductive land grazed by a family of donkeys. Today, the leafy oasis has towering California redwoods beside buttressed kahikatea, spindly kānuka and mānuka, and slow-growing kauri. For over five decades, Dr Alwyn J. Seeley, who owned the gully and whose home overlooked the formerly scrappy landscape, tirelessly helped create a biodiverse, regenerating forest, before gifting the land to the city in 2004. Numerous trails traverse the gully, but an easy route for first-time visitors begins from the stairs on Armagh Street across the creek and left along the pathway to loop back to the start. A short side track leads to a vantage point for views of the wetland.

INFORMATION: Allow 30 to 45 min to explore.

LOCATION: Armagh Street, Hamilton East.

HUNTINGTON

MANGAITI GULLY

Escape the hustle and bustle of city life within this urban gully, a popular outing for families and two-wheeled enthusiasts through regenerating native bush alongside Kirikiriroa Stream. Youngsters on bikes and trikes will enjoy zooming along the wide, mainly flat boardwalks.

Take a breather on the bench seats and watch for kererū/New Zealand pigeon and pīwakawaka/fantails, which often swoop and flit nearby. The stream is part of the Kirikiriroa Gully system stretching from rural hinterlands to the Waikato River near Pukete Bridge.

An easy loop descends a short, steep path into the gully near 53 Keswick Crescent. Keep turning left to return to the trailhead via Helmsdale Court and a short stroll along Keswick Crescent.

INFORMATION: Allow 45 min (about 1.2 km) for the loop.

LOCATION: Keswick Crescent, Huntington.

TE RAPA

PERRY BIKE SKILLS PARK

There's space for riders of all abilities within the park's two main zones. Youngsters still learning the ropes can scoot around the asphalt area with its mini traffic lights and road safety signs, while more confident riders can explore the vast central dirt area with its various trails, or go free-range on the dirt mounds. Near the perimeter, a raised boardwalk tests riders' nerves. Kiwi BMX and track cyclists helped design the custom-built park, handily located beside a café for snacks or coffee.

EXTEND THE ADVENTURE: The nearby Te Awa River Ride (p38) provides longer adventures in the saddle.

INFORMATION: Toilets at the service station, outdoor gym and café. No dogs.

LOCATION: Head north on Te Rapa Road. The service station and bike park are on Hutchinson Road before the SH1 interchange.

BIRD WATCHING

LAKE ROTOROA BIRDLIFE

How many of these birds can you see near the lake?

1. PŪKEKO | PURPLE SWAMP-HEN

Although they're not known for their elegant flying style, pūkeko can still fly long distances and are great swimmers. They mainly eat seeds, roots and shoots, but will chomp down on passing spiders and insects as well. They are widespread, live in permanent social groups and will defend their territory aggressively.

2. CANADA GOOSE

These noisy birds give a loud honk when they're surprised. After they were introduced as a game bird into New Zealand in 1905, their population numbers exploded. By 1996, their estimated population had grown to 40,000 in the South Island, and the bird's protected status was removed in 2011. They like living near lakes or large ponds.

3. KAWAU PŪ | BLACK SHAG

These loners generally forage by themselves and are found from Northland to Bluff. They can weigh more than 2 kilograms, and no one is quite sure how many live in New Zealand; perhaps from 5000 to 10,000 adults. They munch on mainly small to medium-sized fish – less than 35 centimetres in length – including spotties and smelt.

4. AUSTRALIAN COOT

These birds arrived by themselves from Australia and are considered a 'self-introduced' species, which means they are fully protected. They become very territorial during breeding between September and March, so try to avoid disturbing them. They like hanging out on the water and cruise around bobbing their little heads. When frightened, they seek shelter among the reeds.

5. MALLARD DUCK

It's such a Kiwi thing to do – head to the lake to feed the ducks! These introduced birds are probably the ones queuing to take your snacks. About 20 batches of mallards were imported in the 1870s, and now they are one of the most common fowl species in the country. They primarily eat plant material like seeds and grains. Don't feed them bread!

The males have a dark, iridescent-green head and bright yellow bill, while the females (and juveniles) are mottled brown with orange-and-brown bills.

6. KAKĪĀNAU | BLACK SWAN

These graceful birds tend to hang out in pairs, and during breeding will defend their pond patch or lake edge vigorously. They are common throughout New Zealand and mainly live on lakes and larger ponds, and some estuaries. When they fly or lift their wings, you can see their pure-white flight feathers.

image © Hamilton City Council

HAMILTON LAKE DOMAIN

LAKE ROTOROA/HAMILTON LAKE

This central-city lake is a picturesque year-round strolling destination, and the sprawling playground with its water features and climbing tower is ideal for tuckering out the kids.

INFORMATION

GRADE: Easy.

ACCESSIBILITY: Well-graded paths and boardwalks.

TIME: Allow 45 min to 1 hour (about 3.8 km) for the lake loop.

FACILITIES: Toilets, café, picnic tables and playgrounds.

LOCATION: Parking on Rotoroa Drive off Ruakiwi Road.

DOGS: Dogs on leads.

Take a break at the café while the kids tear around the lakeside playground — the water-play feature is a summer highlight (p32). Then, if the family feels sprightly, wander the nearly 4-kilometre loop around the lake past wetlands, home to native and exotic birds — how many are identifiable from the bird guide (p36)? Wide concrete paths are ideal for buggies and wheelchairs, and small jetties provide resting places.

Waikato Hospital dominates the skyline to the south, while on the western side lies Innes Common — playing fields and artificial hockey turfs built on wetlands drained during the 1880s. The common was named after the Innes family, who owned several regional breweries.

About 20,000 years ago, the lake formed when the Waikato River changed course towards Port Waikato instead of near Thames. Peat slowly dammed up the braided river system, gradually increasing the lake's size and current depth, which varies between 2 and 6 metres.

KŪWHARUWHARU
LONGFIN EEL

When eels reach between 25 and 80 years old, they travel 5000 kilometres to breed and lay eggs in the subtropical Pacific Ocean, before dying.

Amazingly, their fertilised eggs drift using ocean currents to reach New Zealand in an epic journey that often takes about 15 months. They transform into glass eels and then elvers before navigating rivers, waterfalls and sometimes dams as they move upstream.

FIND OUT MORE
longfineel.co.nz

FOLLOW THE MIGHTY WAIKATO RIVER

TE AWA RIVER RIDE

Pedal along the country's longest concrete pathway, snaking its way beside the Waikato River from Ngāruawāhia to Karāpiro, past waterfalls, picturesque rural vistas and zigzagging boardwalks before reaching Karāpiro Dam. Here are a few highlights of the trail, which has an overall gentle gradient, making it perfect for all skill levels.
For detailed trail maps, visit te-awa.org.nz.

NGĀRUAWĀHIA TO HOROTIU BRIDGE

This easy section provides a picturesque training ground for kids with its gentle gradient and an opportunity for more experienced riders to clock up some mileage. Highlights include plenty of rural vistas, 3-metre-wide paths and the dramatic 130-metre-long Perry Bridge. Extend the outing by visiting the Perry Bike Skills Park (p35) near Horotiu Bridge and grabbing a snack at the café while the kids tear around.

GRADE: Easiest (Grade 1) to easy (Grade 2).

TIME: Allow 45 min one way.

DISTANCE: 7.5 km one way.

FACILITIES: Toilets and café at Ngāruawāhia and Perry Bike Skills Park.

ACCESSIBILITY: Buggies, bikes and wheelchairs.

LOCATION: Horotiu Bridge Road or Lower Waikato Esplanade, Ngāruawāhia.

DOGS: On leads.

HAMILTON GARDENS TO TAMAHERE VILLAGE

After exploring exotic gardens and cultures at Hamilton Gardens, pedal south to Hammond Park (p24). Here, bikers will need to dismount along the winding, elevated boardwalks beside the Waikato River, but then it's back in the saddle to sidle around bush-clad cliffs and across Mangaonua Gully bridge. Pop out on Riverglade Drive before following Newell Road to Tamahere Village. Refuel the troops and spend some time at the excellent playground before returning the same way or arranging transport home.

GRADE: Easiest (Grade 1) to easy (Grade 2).

TIME: Allow 45 min one way.

DISTANCE: 6.5 km one way.

FACILITIES: Toilets at Hamilton Gardens and Tamahere Village.

ACCESSIBILITY: Buggies, bikes and wheelchairs.

LOCATION: Hamilton Gardens, Cobham Drive.

DOGS: On leads.

GRASSROOTS TRUST VELODROME TO HOOKER ROAD

This fantastic section has everything from river views, waterfalls and picnic tables, to elevated boardwalks. Grab a coffee while peeking inside the velodrome, before hopping on the bikes for a quick, steep descent to the Waikato River, where an impressive boardwalk zigzags its way north beneath towering trees. It's not the flattest of sections, and younger — and older! — riders may need to push their bikes occasionally. But overall, the wide, flowing paths with river views make for a fun, easily accessible family outing. Pack some snacks for the picnic spots along the way.

GRADE: Easy (Grade 2) to intermediate (Grade 3).

TIME: Allow 45 min one way.

DISTANCE: 7.5 km one way.

FACILITIES: Toilets at velodrome.

ACCESSIBILITY: Buggies, bikes and wheelchairs.

LOCATION: Behind Grassroots Trust Velodrome, Cambridge Road.

DOGS: On leads.

GRASSROOTS TRUST VELODROME TO CAMBRIDGE

From the velodrome, the concrete pathway drops sharply to farmland dotted with pūkeko as it makes its way over small wooden bridges towards the Waikato River. The broad path is ideal for riding alongside little kids still earning their stripes on two wheels. It's also popular with runners and walkers, so keep an eye out for other users. Pedal through a swathe of fertile countryside and past the remnants of a pā once surrounded by sprawling kūmara and yam gardens before reaching the Gaslight Theatre at Cambridge. From the theatre, it's an additional couple of kilometres into the centre of Cambridge with its cafés and ice cream shops.

GRADE: Easy (Grade 2).

TIME: Allow 30 min one way.

DISTANCE: 3.5 km one way to the Gaslight Theatre.

FACILITIES: Toilets at velodrome.

ACCESSIBILITY: Buggies, bikes and wheelchairs.

LOCATION: Velodrome, Cambridge Road or Gaslight Theatre on Alpha Street.

DOGS: On leads.

CAMBRIDGE TO LAKE KARĀPIRO

An easy trail follows the main road from the outskirts of Cambridge to the Mighty River Domain at Lake Karāpiro, where there's a playground for kids and a café to grab a coffee and a bite to eat. Bikers won't break a sweat pedalling along the wide, flat pathway as it passes rural scenery alongside horse studs, typical of the region's landscape. Before dipping down the short hill to the Karāpiro Dam, there are great views of Lake Karāpiro and Maungatautari Mountain in the distance. Visit during rowing regattas and perch on the large, grassy banks to soak up the spectacle as teams battle it out on the water.

GRADE: Easiest (Grade 1) to easy (Grade 2).

TIME: Allow 45 min one way.

DISTANCE: 8 km one way.

FACILITIES: Toilets and cafés in Cambridge and at Mighty River Domain.

ACCESSIBILITY: Buggies, bikes and wheelchairs.

LOCATION: Parking on Carlyle Street, Cambridge.

DOGS: On leads. No dogs in domain.

LAKE KARĀPIRO TO ROWING START LINE

The final section of the Te Awa River Ride is a short section taking riders from the Mighty River Domain to the rowing starting line, but prepare yourself for a short, gut-busting hill. From the domain, head south along Maungatautari Road on a relatively flat concrete trail until 'the hill'. Even the hardiest cyclists might have to dismount and push their bikes. But the rewards are worth it for views along the lake, which has become the breeding ground for Olympic champions. The trail ends after a long, twisty boardwalk perched over the river. It's an excellent addition to an afternoon spent at the domain.

GRADE: Easy (Grade 2).

TIME: Allow 20 min one way.

DISTANCE: 2 km one way.

FACILITIES: Toilets and cafés at Mighty River Domain. Ice cream stall on Maungatautari Road.

ACCESSIBILITY: Buggies, bikes and wheelchairs.

LOCATION: Mighty River Domain, Karāpiro.

DOGS: On leads. No dogs in domain.

image © Gary Clare

SH3 TE AWAMUTU

YARNDLEY'S BUSH

Step back in time to when vast swamps covered the region and flying dinosaurs swooped down to nibble on the fleshy seeds of kahikatea trees, during the Jurassic period.

INFORMATION

GRADE: Easy.

ACCESSIBILITY: Boardwalks, grass and dirt paths.

TIME: Allow 30 to 45 min for the loop.

FACILITIES: None.

LOCATION: Turn off SH3 onto Ngāroto Road between Hamilton and Te Awamutu. The entrance is about 1.4 km on the left; but the car park is a further 180 metres on the right.

DOGS: Dogs on leads.

Navigate a strip of sloping pasture before arriving at the forest edge. Upon entering, a looping pathway disappears into the dark forest, and it's easy to imagine how the landscape looked during prehistoric times. Unfortunately, only 120 hectares of this important swamp forest remains in the Waipā district today, so preserving this 14-hectare remnant is significant.

Boardwalks wind past kahikatea-root buttresses rising from the ground, surrounded by regenerating native plants thriving on the forest floor. Many kahikatea became 'perched' above the ground after the peat shrunk when swamp forests were drained, exposing their impressive roots.

Approximately halfway around the loop, a viewing tower disappears skyward into the trees. Clamber up the stairs for views of the forest; on windy days, kids can lie on the seating platform and listen to the trees creating spooky, creaking sounds while swaying above them.

Plenty of signs along the way provide an overview of the

plants and critters in this soggy environment — look for tuna/eels hiding in the small stream beside the boardwalk.

The wide, winding boardwalk continues past giant kahikatea, some more than 35 metres tall. They are the nation's tallest native tree, often seen poking through lowland forest canopies.

ACCESSIBILITY

Buggies may need to be lifted over the tight entryway before a moderately steep grassed slope, suiting outdoorsy buggies.

WHAT LIVES IN
THE WAIKATO RIVER?

There's plenty happening just below the surface of this 425-kilometre-long river as it makes its way from Lake Taupō to the wild Tasman Sea at Port Waikato. Native eels jostle for space with introduced fish, while kōura/freshwater crayfish and native kōuraura/shrimp lurk in the shallows.

CATFISH
INTRODUCED

RAINBOW TROUT – INTRODUCED

KŪWHARUWHARU
NATIVE LONGFIN EEL

GOLDFISH – INTRODUCED

BLACK MUDFISH
NATIVE

GAMBUSIA | MOSQUITOFISH – INTRODUCED

image © Keri Neilson

ŌHAUPŌ

LAKE ROTOPIKO

Protected by a predator-proof fence, this 18,000-year-old peat lake has an easy trail looping around its shoreline with plenty of activities to keep the kids entertained.

INFORMATION

GRADE: Easy.

ACCESSIBILITY: Boardwalks, grass and dirt paths. Doable with outdoorsy buggies if feeling energetic.

TIME: Allow 1 hour for the loop.

FACILITIES: Rustic toilet, picnic tables.

LOCATION: 4 km south of Ōhaupō. The entrance is accessible southbound only on SH3 between Sowerby and Jary Roads.

DOGS: No dogs.

Grab a trail map near the entrance of the pest-proof enclosure — after making sure no pesky rodents have hitchhiked through in bags — and follow the mown grassy trail to the Lake Circuit sign. Walking clockwise is recommended to tick off the fun activities.

From the pontoon, scout for critters darting through the waters or look for the mysterious pūweto/spotless crake making a rare appearance near the shoreline. Then, at the Eels and Ladders game, see the length of one huge endangered native tuna kūwharuwharu/longfin eel — yikes!

The boardwalk sidles past regenerating native trees and a wooden viewing platform, towards the home of possibly the world's teeniest caterpillar, Fred the Thread (p29). Look for the wiggly lines it makes on the giant cane rush stems.

JURASSIC LOOP

The Jurassic Loop is a fun 10-minute detour through a stand of lofty kahikatea trees with wizened buttresses looming from the ground. However, this section isn't buggy-friendly.

TAMAHERE

TAMAHERE RESERVE

For 30 years, this rare remnant of lowland kahikatea swamp forest had become a neglected wasteland rife with pest plants and animals. Yet since 2012, Leo Koppens and numerous volunteers have been transforming the gully to its former glory.

Negotiate the steep path shaded by pine trees into the reserve. Long boardwalks and well-graded dirt paths wind past exotic trees providing cover for regenerating mamaku, māhoe, carex grasses and ponga. Some stands of trees are more than 400 years old.

Viewing platforms overlook the meandering Mangaone Stream and its resident tuna/eels.

INFORMATION: Allow 1 hour to explore. Suitable for walking only. Dogs on leads.

LOCATION: Car park on Tauwhare Road, opposite Woodcock Road.

TAMAHERE

ALLAN TURNER WALKWAY

This swaying suspension bridge spanning the Mangaharakeke Stream provides a short, entertaining adventure for when the troops get cabin fever. Explore the bridge before disappearing down the dirt nature trail at the Woodcock Road bridge end to the regenerating gully and walk beside the stream. Brave kids can clamber across the nearby crisscrossing narrow wooden planks.

Pekapeka-tou-roa/long-tailed bats use the gully as a 'green corridor' linking swathes of green space within the region, including Maungatautari and Mount Pirongia.

Volunteers are extending the pathway — find out more tamaherewalkways.org.

INFORMATION: Allow 5 to 30 min return. Full accessibility on the bridge. Walking only for the nature trail. Dogs on leads.

LOCATION: Parking is available at both Woodcock Road and Fuchsia Lane.

TE AWAMUTU

LAKE NGĀ ROTO

Combine a leisurely stroll or bike ride with a cultural and conservation tour while visiting this natural wetland. Plenty of information signs dotted along the path provide information on the peat lake, the largest in the Waipā district, and offer a quick breather while adventuring.

For a detailed history of the nearby Taurangamirumiru pā, the lives of the tīpuna/Māori ancestors who lived there, the battle of Hingakākā, and the ecology and restoration of the area, there are excellent resources at tearawai.nz.

The loop has well-graded dirt paths and many kilometres of boardwalk through diverse landscapes. Beside the car park and shoreline, large grassy areas are good for picnics and kicking/throwing balls.

INFORMATION: Allow 1 hour to 90 min (about 6 km) for the loop and tour; 30 min for biking (follow the directional signs). Toilets available. Dogs on leads.

LOCATION: From SH3, follow Ngāroto Road onto Pāterangi Road, then Bank Road. Plenty of parking.

TE MIRO

TE MIRO MTB PARK

A tangled network of mountain bike trails traverses sloping hillsides surrounding a picturesque reservoir between Cambridge and Morrinsville.

About 30 kilometres of trails wind beneath sprawling exotic and native forest, with some excellent options for kids progressing onto dirt trails. Post-ride, enjoy lazing on the large grassy banks leading down to the water's edge or cook some sausages on the barbecue.

WHERE TO START?

For a family-friendly ride with plenty of highlights, Big Willy is an excellent first-timers' trail. Allow about 10 to 25 minutes for the gently undulating two-way loop, and if anyone gets tuckered out you can quickly retreat. Keep an eye out for bikers coming from all directions. At The Lookout, take a breather and enjoy the views. The 2-kilometre-long trail begins below the main car park on a series of switchbacks leading down the slope.

The Snake trail and Big Red are also close to the car park and ideal for more experienced kids. Other intermediate-grade trails include Easy Flows It and Gobblers Knob.

TE MIRO MTB CLUB

This enthusiastic club caters to all abilities and has a range of events for all ages and abilities. Kids keen to learn new trail skills will enjoy the regular workshops — check the club website for dates. Annual individual and family memberships are available. Memberships help the club build and maintain trails and the park's facilities. Check out the website for more information and trail maps.

FIND OUT MORE
temiromtbclub.co.nz

INFORMATION

FACILITIES: Toilets, shelter, covered barbecue area and water supply.

TRAIL GRADES: Grade 2 (easy) through to Grade 5 (expert).

OPENING HOURS: Riders can access the park 24 hours.

ENTRANCE FEE: Free, although donating to Te Miro MTB Club helps maintain the tracks.

ARE E-BIKES ALLOWED? Yes.

ARE DOGS ALLOWED? Dogs are discouraged for safety reasons.

IS RUNNING OR WALKING ALLOWED? Not on the trails.

LOCATION: The main car park is on Waterworks Road, Te Miro.

TE AWAMUTU

KAKEPUKU TRACK

Clambering up an extinct volcano is no easy feat, but, luckily, excellent views from an abandoned pā on its summit compensate for burning lungs. Before the path begins to switch-back gently up the mountainside, gradually getting steeper and more taxing, a short farmland section and viewing platform provide a bird's-eye view of the surrounding countryside. Ferns shade the steepening trail and a short flat section, which briefly provides some respite before the final push up multiple stairways to the trig. The pā site has commanding views at 449 metres above sea level. On clear days, take in the sights of the Waikato Basin and Mount Ruapehu on the southern horizon. A short boardwalk continues past the trig and loops back to the main path.

INFORMATION: Allow 2 to 3 hours return. No dogs. Clay paths can become slippery in winter. A Grade 2 (easy) mountain bike trail shares the lower three-quarters of the trail. Toilet near the trailhead.

LOCATION: Car park on Kakepuku Road.

MAUNGATAUTARI MOUNTAIN

TE ARA TIROHIA LOOP TRACK

Tucked away on the northern flanks of Maungatautari, this small forest surrounded by a predator-proof enclosure is part of the larger 3400-hectare ecological 'island' on this prominent maunga.

Native plants and birdlife thrive alongside the nearly 1-kilometre-long trail passing beneath mature native trees and across forest streams, with scooting little aquatic critters. Fallen trees allow budding botanists to examine different fungus types.

From the car park, walk to the end of Hicks Road and follow the well-signposted path beside pasture to the forest line. The entrance gate is further to the right.

INFORMATION: Allow 1 hour return. Walking only. No dogs. No entry fee.

LOCATION: Parking beside Maungatautari Pā, Hicks Road. About 15 minutes from Cambridge.

CAMBRIDGE

LAKE TE KOO UTU

Below Cambridge township there is a popular wide, flat pathway that loops around the shoreline of a picturesque lake surrounded by steep tree-clad slopes.

Established in 1880 by the Cambridge Domain Board, the 17-hectare reserve is full of mature trees for shady respite during balmy summer days. Numerous tracks detour from the lakeside loop. Although most are not buggy-friendly, they offer a good workout — try to find the cascading water feature. Tree boffins will enjoy looking for rare species growing along the pathway.

Nearby on Thornton Road is a playground and a sweltering tropical-plant glasshouse.

INFORMATION: Allow 30 to 45 min (about 1 km) for the loop. Toilet and barbecue near the car park. Dogs on leads. No bikes.

LOCATION: Main car park entrance off Albert Street.

image © Pirongia MTB Club

PIRONGIA

MOUNT PIRONGIA MTB TRAILS

Winding through forestry blocks covering Mount Pirongia is a network of accessible, family-friendly mountain bike trails, suiting all ages and abilities.

After more than a decade of building trails, the Pirongia Mountain Bike Club now has about 14 kilometres of excellent, flowy jump trails, technical downhills and smooth-sailing single trails. So it doesn't matter if the kids are beginners or have some miles in the saddle, bring the bikes and enjoy some two-wheeling adventures.

WHERE TO START?

From the lower car park, jump on the out-and-back Home and Away trail, which heads north along the forest's perimeter. This trail is rideable in both directions, so if the kids run out of steam, everyone can turn around and head back to the car. Newly minted riders will enjoy testing their wheels on the well-groomed trail. For a longer adventure, at the northern end of Home and Away, loop back on the well-signposted forestry road before using the Joining Link to connect with southern trails, The Apprentice and Easy As, back to the car park.

Allow 20 min (3 km) return for Home and Away and 30 min (4 km) to complete the entire loop.

PIRONGIA MTB CLUB

This active club, formerly known as the Waipā MTB Club, was formed in 2008 and regularly hosts events for a wide range of riding types and skill levels. New trails are constantly under development, and the club appreciates keen volunteers lending a hand with track-building and general maintenance.

On Thursdays, the club has regular rides from Pirongia. Check out the website for more information and trail maps.

FIND OUT MORE
pirongiamtb.co.nz

INFORMATION

FACILITIES: Toilet and shelter. No water. Cell-phone coverage is patchy.

TRAIL GRADES: Grade 2 (easy) through to Grade 5 (expert).

OPENING HOURS: Riders can access the park 24 hours.

ENTRANCE FEE: There is no cost to use the forest; however, donating to the club is appreciated.

ARE E-BIKES ALLOWED? Yes.

ARE DOGS ALLOWED? Dogs are discouraged for safety reasons.

IS RUNNING OR WALKING ALLOWED? Not on the trails.

LOCATION: From Pirongia, cross the Waipā River onto O'Shea Road, then turn left up Sainsbury Road. Follow for 5 km.

LET LOOSE ON

WAIPĀ PLAYGROUNDS

CAMBRIDGE

ST KILDA PLAYGROUND

Older kids can practise their free throws on the basketball court or tear around the bumpy cycle path on their scooters, while younger kids will enjoy the basket swing and small slides. Plenty of nature-based elements to clamber over and explore.

LOCATION: Parking on Kaniera Terrace.

TE AWAMUTU

PIONEER PARK

Settle in for an afternoon exhausting the kids in this sprawling park catering to all ages with its water-play area, picnic tables, bike-skills park and slides zipping down the hillside. Toddlers will enjoy the colourful, fenced preschoolers' space.

LOCATION: Parking on Gorst Avenue near the Te Awamutu Rose Garden.

image © Waipā District Council

TAMAHERE

TAMAHERE PARK

Massive wide slides, rope-climbing frames, a half basketball court, skate park, mini-trampolines, rope-climbing structures and balance equipment should tucker out even the hardiest playground-goer.

LOCATION: Parking beside Tamahere Village on Wiremu Tāmihana Drive.

CAMBRIDGE

LEAMINGTON DOMAIN MINIATURE TRAIN

Train enthusiasts will love the miniature trains chugging around on the first and third Sunday of each month, weather permitting. Grab a ride between 10am and 2pm. Rides cost $2 per person, under-fives free. Covered-toe shoes are required.

LOCATION: Wordsworth Street, Leamington.

CAMBRIDGE

THOMPSON STREET PLAYGROUND

Combine a play on the looping bike track, swings, climbing frames, hut and flying fox with a stroll or bike along the town-belt walking trail.

LOCATION: Thompson Street, Leamington.

image © Waipā District Council

ON TWO WHEELS

WAIPĀ BIKE ADVENTURES

Saddle up for some of the region's coolest bike parks, including one of the largest pump tracks in Oceania, or learn essential road skills tootling around colourful bike-skills parks. No matter how experienced the family are on two wheels, there's something for everyone.

CAMBRIDGE

GALLAGHER BIKE SKILLS PARK

This purpose-built park has enough to entertain aspiring mountain bikers of all ages and abilities. Older kids can happily freewheel along the smooth concrete paths and curved wooden boardwalks winding through native shrubs with a picturesque backdrop of farmland. Nearby, little kids on balance bikes, scooters and pedal bikes can learn essential road skills by pottering along the bike-skills park, with its traffic lights, roundabouts and road signs. Afterwards, grab a coffee and snack at the nearby café and chill out by the Perry Playground. A short, well-hidden MTB trail also connects with Te Awa River Trail (p38) — the trailhead is near the fence on the southern side of the velodrome.

INFORMATION: Drinking fountain. Café and toilets at the velodrome.

LOCATION: Parking behind the velodrome off Hanlin Road.

CAMBRIDGE

PUMP TRACK AND SKATE PARK

Keen skaters and riders can rail some berms or nail an ollie during an afternoon of fun on one of the largest pump tracks in Oceania. Enjoy serious thrills on the bowl connecting the smooth-flowing 196-metre-long pump track and fun 222-metre-long jump track covering more than 2300 m². It's a popular destination for out-of-town riders.

Its scenic position beside the Waikato River, near an impressive skate park and swimming pools, mean once you've worked up a sweat and tested some riding skills, you can cool off with a dip.

INFORMATION: Drinking fountain and toilet beside the car park.

LOCATION: Parking on Dominion Avenue, Cambridge.

TE AWAMUTU

CENTENNIAL PARK

Bring the teenagers and skateboards because this park has all the rims, rails and bowls needed for perfecting grinds and grabbing some airtime. Then feel the flow of the parkour course while freerunning and challenging buddies in pursuit of the fastest, most efficient ways to navigate the obstacles. Or, if that sounds exhausting, chill in the shaded hang-out zone before shooting a few hoops on the basketball court. An undulating, winding concrete trail loops around the park for bikes and scooters. There's enough to entertain older kids, but a small playground will tempt little adventurers, too.

INFORMATION: Drinking fountain and toilet beside the car park.

LOCATION: Parking on Rewi Street, Te Awamutu.

PIRONGIA FOREST PARK

NĪKAU WALK AND KĀNIWHANIWHA CAVES

This outing ticks all the boxes if the kids are not squeamish about underground caves and unnervingly close cave wētā encounters.

Follow alongside the burbling, clear waters of the Kāniwhaniwha Stream, sometimes with the occasional angler attempting to catch dinner, on an easy, flat 4WD trail to the forested edge of Pirongia Forest Park. The path enters the forest at the junction, weaving beneath tall palms as it follows the Nīkau Walk loop.

A 30-minute detour to Kāniwhaniwha Caves — the only limestone caves in the forest park — leads to two caves. The largest and most kid-friendly is the signposted 20-metre-long cave. Although parts of the often muddy, damp cave reach 7.5 metres high, there are a couple of relatively snug corners to navigate. A torch makes this adventure safer and more enjoyable — look for ocean-dwelling fossils trapped for millions of years in the limestone walls. Get up close and personal with wētā hanging out on the walls while splashing through the cave.

Clamber up the wooden ladder at the end of the cave before returning to the Nīkau Walk. Then, continue along the trail to a grassy campsite (part of the Te Araroa Trail) with toilets, before connecting with the 4WD path back to the car park.

KĀNIWHANIWHA RESERVE

After adventuring, laze around on the grass beside the car park beside the shallow stream. Ideal for washing off cave dirt and letting the kids have a paddle. Toilets are available.

MOUNTAIN BIKING

The Nīkau Walk is dual-use, with mountain bikers (Grade 1/easiest) and walkers enjoying the trail. However, bikes are not allowed on the detour to Kāniwhaniwha Caves.

EXTEND YOUR ADVENTURE

Walk to the tallest recorded native tree in New Zealand, a soaring 66.5-metre-high kahikatea. From Kāniwhaniwha Reserve, allow 6 hours return for this 12-kilometre-long adventure. The trail is suitable for older kids as it can get muddy. The trail is signposted near the caves.

INFORMATION

GRADE: Easy or Medium.

ACCESSIBILITY: Well-graded 4WD track, dirt paths, boardwalks and narrow, dark caves. Suitable for buggies and bikes to the grassy picnic area but not on the loop.

TIME: Allow 150 min (7 km) return for the loop and caves.

FACILITIES: Toilets available.

LOCATION: Limeworks Loop Road near Te Pahū.

DOGS: No dogs.

HAVE YOU SEEN A BIRD OF PREY?

New Zealand has three native raptors. The term 'raptor' comes from the Latin word *rapere*, which means 'to snatch or take away'. These birds use their feet to catch their prey, and their hooked beak helps them eat bite-sized pieces of their catch.

KĀREAREA | NEW ZEALAND FALCON

Falcons are capable of flying at speeds over 100 kilometres an hour and are often seen flying in active chase rather than slowly swooping around like the harrier. They kill their prey with a quick bite to the neck, and their diet mainly consists of birds but also insects.

KĀHU | SWAMP HARRIER

Harriers like to feed on road kill and are often spotted perched on roadside fences. Possums, rabbits and hedgehogs make up a large part of their diet. They are opportunistic hunters while flying lazily and are the country's largest bird of prey.

RURU | MOREPORK

By day they roost in the cavities of trees, and at night they hunt for beetles, wētā, moths and spiders. At dusk, you can often hear their haunting call, and during the night they can be heard in many urban parks and leafy suburbs.

PIRONGIA FOREST PARK
RUAPANE LOOKOUT

Enjoy clambering up the side of a volcano across tangled tree roots and steep rock formations? Then your bucket list just got longer. But despite it being a grunty adventure to scale the exposed rocky outcrop with its wooden trig, the views across the Waikato from the 723-metre-high vantage spot are worthwhile.

From the car park, the steps begin immediately, with only a few flattish sections providing some respite. Bring snacks and hydration for the steady climb through the native forest to the summit. After the steps, the path turns into a rough tramping track best avoided during winter or after heavy rain, as it can become a boggy mess.

Pop little ones into a backpack if feeling extremely fit, as this walk mainly suits older children.

INFORMATION: Allow up to 3 hours return. Toilet beside the car park. No dogs.

LOCATION: End of Corcoran Road near Te Pahū.

PIRONGIA FOREST PARK
MOUNT PIRONGIA

If the family has ticked off the forest park's shorter bushwalks, set everyone's sights on the summit of this magnificent maunga.

Folks keen to head into the challenging interior of this forest park should prepare themselves for gut-busting climbs towards its 959-metre-high peak. Multiple routes ascend its flanks; some day-hikes are meandering, while others offer more strenuous outings. All options require a reasonable standard of fitness and tramping experience.

Or split up the trip by staying at the bookable 20-bunk Pāhautea Hut near the summit, an achievable destination for young hikers.

Listen out for the haunting birdsong of the at-risk kōkako, reintroduced to the forest park in 2017.

INFORMATION: Find out more doc.govt.nz.

LOCATION: Multiple access points.

PIRONGIA
ALEXANDRA REDOUBT

Tucked behind the small settlement of Pirongia, this well-preserved redoubt is a worthy detour. Constructed in 1872, the redoubt shares the township's former name. European settlers had urged officials to provide the redoubt in case Waikato Māori, forced south after the government seized tribal land, returned to claim their homelands. Similar fortifications were built across the district, but this is the best-preserved example of these military earthworks.

Cross the small footbridge over the fortification ditch into the main area, which once housed barracks and a flagstaff. Take care not to walk on the escarpment walls.

An excellent Waikato War Driving Tour audio tour is available at thewaikatowar.co.nz.

INFORMATION: Allow 15 min to explore. Walking only. No dogs.

LOCATION: Bellot Street in Pirongia.

PIRONGIA FOREST PARK

MANGAKARA NATURE WALK

Looping along the fringes of Pirongia Forest Park, this kid-friendly outing has streams for playing Poohsticks, a mysterious boulder and a dose of education with its nature trail — an excellent half-day adventure.

INFORMATION

GRADE: Easy.

ACCESSIBILITY: Well-graded paths, steps and boardwalks.

TIME: Allow 1 hour for a relaxed loop stroll — more if avidly reading the signs.

FACILITIES: Toilets near the car park.

LOCATION: From Hamilton, travel west towards Te Pahū and turn onto Rosborough Road, then Grey Road.

DOGS: No dogs.

Winding through an ancient forest, this nature trail is far enough away from Hamilton city to feel like an intrepid adventure but close enough to be easily accessible. And, with boardwalks snaking beneath and through stands of native trees and past meandering streams, there's enough to keep kids entertained for a couple of hours. Look for suitable floating twigs along the way to challenge the family to a game of Poohsticks on the bridges.

Then there's the unmissable mysterious slab of rock. This climbable grey boulder has perplexed many boffins who have debated whether it was ejected by a volcano or perhaps, because of its round surface, it may have tumbled down a river.

Approximately three-quarters of the way around the loop, a small seating area beside the stream is an excellent spot for a bite to eat and a paddle in summer. Bring insect repellent if planning to loiter, as limbs won't escape unscathed when active biters are around. Peer into the clear stream for insects hiding beside the rocks, an important food source for kōkopu. Kōura/freshwater crayfish and tuna/eels can often be spotted swimming and crawling through the slow-moving water.

NATURE TRAIL

Download a Department of Conservation fact sheet matching the nature trail's numbered posts for a healthy dose of flora and fauna education. Visit doc.govt.nz.

LOOKOUT

A small lookout near the toilet has impressive Waikato Basin views.

WHATAWHATA

KARAKARIKI TRACK

Feel like fossicking for fossils? Look for ancient sea creatures and shells at this popular summer swimming hole only 20 minutes from Hamilton.

INFORMATION

GRADE: Easy.

ACCESSIBILITY: Mix of dirt and grass paths. Stiles to cross.

TIME: Allow 1 hour for a quick out-and-back or longer for picnics and toe-dipping.

FACILITIES: No toilets.

LOCATION: 5 min past Whatawhata on SH23, turn onto Karakariki Road, then left at Karakariki Christian Camp onto Karakariki Valley Road.

DOGS: No dogs.

Cascading down exposed rocks, Karakariki Waterfall creates a shallow swimming hole popular with little kids for paddling, while its rock ledges are launching pads for older kids. Bonus, the occasional fossil dating back millions of years lurks in the shallow streambed.

From the car park, cross the suspension bridge across Karakariki Stream onto farmland. Continue past regenerating trees and shrubs growing beside the stream before a short, steep clamber down to the streambed and picnicking area beside the waterfall. Alternatively, cross the stream earlier at the 4WD crossing and walk along the opposite bank to avoid scrambling down the bank.

Please don't disturb any livestock, and avoid the electric fences. In winter, this becomes a fun but muddy adventure; perhaps bring a spare set of clothes for afterwards.

KAWAKAWA

Rongoā/Māori medicinal practices have used heart-shaped kawakawa leaves for many years. Its mildly antiseptic and pain-numbing properties have been used to treat eczema, toothache, wounds and abscesses through to kidney and stomach problems.

Ever wondered why some of the slightly peppery, bitter-tasting leaves have more holes? The most potent and tastiest leaves attract the kawakawa looper moth, which munches through them.

OLD MOUNTAIN ROAD

MANGAKIRIRI LOOP TRACK

Follow a bush-clad ridgeline as it climbs to a vantage point with views across the Waikato Basin — an excellent adventure for families seeking a gradient-filled outing!

INFORMATION

GRADE: Medium/Hard.

ACCESSIBILITY: Mix of dirt and grass paths. Steep gradients. Follow the yellow track-markers.

TIME: Allow 100 min return with a steady pace.

FACILITIES: Toilet near the car park. Picnic table.

LOCATION: Ed Hillary Hope Reserve, Old Mountain Road, near Whatawhata.

DOGS: No dogs.

Starting from Ed Hillary Hope Reserve, the trail climbs steadily beneath a canopy of tānekaha/celery pine. Large loops of climbing rātā vines grow beside the path, attempting to latch onto trunks and reach sunlight above the treetops.

Although not marked near the top, a well-trodden path leads to the viewpoint on the right. It's worth the short detour if only for a quick rest. Then it's downhill back to a 4WD trail leading to the car park. Although the walk is steep in a few places, it's a doable adventure with children, if not rushing. Little kids might be best in backpacks.

ED HILLARY HOPE RESERVE

This 460-hectare reserve is part of the Hamilton Halo project, helping to bring native birds such as tūī and korimako/bellbird back to the city. Restoring the former erosion-prone grassland has allowed tōtara, rimu, rewarewa and kāmahi to thrive. In late summer, large flocks of kererū/New Zealand pigeons congregate to feed on tawa and miro fruits.

SHORTER ADVENTURE

The Valley Walk is an easy, 30-minute out-and-back adventure along a 4WD path through the lower valley, which would suit younger children. Follow the orange track-markers from the car park.

WAIRĒINGA/BRIDAL VEIL FALLS | NEAR RAGLAN

TE MATA | RAGLAN

WAIRĒINGA | BRIDAL VEIL FALLS

Legend says this bush-clad valley is home to mist-dwelling fairies who seduce travellers with their musical prowess.

INFORMATION

GRADE: Easy/Medium.

ACCESSIBILITY: Mix of dirt paths and steps.

TIME: 20 min return to the lookout (buggy-friendly); 1 hour return (walking only) to the base of the falls.

FACILITIES: Toilet near the car park.

LOCATION: From Hamilton, travel west towards Raglan on SH23 and turn onto Te Mata Road after Te Uku. Follow the signs.

DOGS: No dogs.

Reaching the base of this impressive 55-metre-high waterfall means navigating 261 steps plummeting down a hillside. Luckily, for younger explorers or those feeling less energetic, views of the Pakoka River's dramatic detour on its journey to Aotea Harbour can be seen from two easily accessible viewing platforms perched on the upper edge of the lava flow.

But for the complete package of towering raw rock views and misty rainbows, make the trek to the lower bridge at the base of the falls. Take a breather at the nīkau-shrouded mid-way point and look for the reserve's unique spider orchid. Then at the bottom bridge, the hard basalt rock forming the lip of the falls becomes visible, formed when a nearby volcano erupted 2.5 million years ago, spewing molten rock down a river channel, which cooled and eventually stopped flowing.

A shelter provides a good picnic area, and information panels explain the area's geology.

LAKE DISAPPEAR

A further 2.7 kilometres south past Wairēinga/Bridal Veil Falls on Kāwhia Road is a valley with an underground network of occasionally waterlogged caves, creating an impressive but temporary glistening lake surrounded by paddocks. Unfortunately, this quirky geological feature lives up to its name, but after prolonged rain you may see where an ancient lava flow has diverted the course of Pakihi Stream into a limestone sinkhole before flowing underground through a cave system for a few kilometres.

RAGLAN

MOUNT KARIOI

Summit this ancient volcano for spectacular views of Waikato, the Tasman Sea and south to Taranaki and Pureora Forest Park. Two tracks lead to the mountain summit, and although this option is steeper — with the occasional chain and ladder across rocky outcrops — it's more interesting and closer to Raglan than the Karioi Road alternative. The trail starts opposite the Te Toto Gorge car park, where it's all uphill to the main ridge. After reaching the lookout, it's another hour to the summit. On a fine day, the views are well worth the effort.

ACCESSIBILITY: Hard adventure with dirt paths, stiles, rocks and grassy slopes.

INFORMATION: For the latest trail updates, visit doc.govt.nz.

LOCATION: Head south through Raglan on Wainui Road, then Whaanga Road. Parking is at the signposted Te Toto Gorge, about 13 km from Raglan. Last 4 km on gravel.

RAGLAN

WAINUI RESERVE BUSH PARK

When the summer sun is sizzling, escape into this shady 10-hectare bush reserve with its winding paths and shaded streams. The Friends of Wainui Bush Reserve have cultivated this area from a former farm into a thriving bird habitat. The green space also adjoins a large farm park overlooking the rugged Tasman Sea coastline. A kid-friendly option to a vantage point above the wild west coast is along the Ridge Walk, over the stile and across farmland to the coastline — look for frolicking Māui dolphins (p15) offshore. There's no shade on this trail section so remember to slip, slop, slap and wrap.

INFORMATION: Easy to medium. Optional steep ridgeline walk. Allow 1 hour to explore both areas. Recommend taking a photo of the trail map by the car park. Toilet near the trailhead. Dogs on leads.

LOCATION: Head south from Raglan. Car park opposite 349 Wainui Road.

RAGLAN

SEASIDE BOARDWALK

Grab an ice cream from parlours touting their tasty treats on the main street, then head to the shoreline and turn right. This short, fun boardwalk adventure hugging the water's edge is a good length for young explorers on foot, in buggies or on two wheels.

Keep a watchful eye across Whāingaroa/Raglan Harbour for the critically endangered Māui dolphin, which has visited the harbour. The 12-kilometre-long harbour, with its tidal lagoon and drowned river valley, is deceptively large, with a shoreline of more than 140 kilometres.

Once you've had your fill of salty sea air and harbour views, return the same way or take the stairs onto Cliff Street and stroll back into town.

INFORMATION: Allow 15 min return. Suitable for walking, buggies and wheelchairs. Dogs on leads.

LOCATION: Accessible from the end of Bow Street.

RAGLAN

TE TOTO GORGE

Explore a windswept gorge beside the wild Tasman Sea, or test the nerves on a viewing platform dangling over a cliff.

INFORMATION

GRADE: Hard.

ACCESSIBILITY: Steep slopes, rocks, roots and tricky spots to navigate. Slippery in winter.

TIME: Allow 150 min return to the shoreline and back. More if dawdling or exploring the rocks.

FACILITIES: No toilets.

LOCATION: Head south from Raglan on Wainui Road, then Whaanga Road. Parking is at the signposted Te Toto Gorge, about 13 km from Raglan. Last 4 km on gravel.

DOGS: Dogs on leads.

Although this is a great half-day outing for adventurous families, prepare yourself; from the car park, the trail descends a steep, uneven ridge before navigating rocks and ankle-grabbing roots. Luckily, stopping to look at dozens of kōwhai trees filled with tuneful tūī provides a breather. Then, dense grass must be navigated when things flatten out in the gorge. It's an adventure!

Take a breather near the edge of the coastal amphitheatre, where the booming surf is impressive, or add another 30 minutes (return) to clamber down to the rocky shoreline for some salty spray. Take care navigating the path, as one of the country's most threatened native coastal plants grow here: Cook's scurvy grass. To the north, the 150-metre-high cliffs were formed by multiple lava flows from the 2.4-million-year-old volcano Karioi.

From the car park, walk about 15 metres north towards Raglan. There's no sign, and the dirt track takes some hunting to find in the trees — look for the orange triangle markers. At the bottom, take a photo of the bush exit to make it easier for the return trip. Or follow the stream back into the bush to locate the trail. For this isolated walk, hikers must be reasonably confident following track markings.

MĀORI HISTORY

In the 1700s, the gorge was the site of expansive Māori gardens. There are still remnants of two small pā/fortified villages, including terraces, storage pits and rows of stone that outlined plots.

WILD WEST TASMAN SEA

RAGLAN'S BEACHES

A trip to Raglan is not complete without some black-sand action, so tempt the family with these five kid-friendly beaches — from shallow pools to wallow in at low tide to boulder-strewn coastlines perfect for rock-hopping.

NGARUNUI | OCEAN BEACH

Patrolled by surf lifesavers during high season, this vast beach is very popular, with hordes of families descending upon its black sands in summer to swim, sunbathe and learn to surf. Careful: black sand becomes blistering hot mid-summer.

INFORMATION: Toilets, showers and changing facilities. Head south from Raglan on Wainui Road for about 5 km.

TE KOPUA BEACH

Cross the footbridge at the end of Bow Street to spend an afternoon wallowing in the estuary waters and watching folks leaping off the bridge, or bring kayaks for a sheltered paddle.

INFORMATION: Toilets, food outlets, playground, skate park and water fountain. Access from the end of Bow Street or Marine Parade.

WAINAMU BEACH

A sprawling stretch of sand near the entrance of Whāingaroa/ Raglan Harbour. At low tide shallow pools remain, which are toasty warm during summer for paddling in. This beach connects to Ngarunui.

INFORMATION: Toilets, showers and changing facilities. Head south from Raglan on Wainui Road for about 4 km. Turn right onto Riria Kereopa Memorial Drive.

WHALE BAY

This beach best suits hard-core surfers, but it's fun to perch on the weird and wonderfully shaped rocks to watch the surfing action and spectacular sunsets. Kids can peer into the rock pools looking for critters.

INFORMATION: Toilets, nearby playground and picnic area. Head south from Raglan on Wainui Road for about 8 km, then turn onto Calvert Road.

RUAPUKE BEACH

For fewer crowds and more wild, windswept action, continue south to this sweeping beach beside the Tasman Sea. Its remote location means the beach is often unpopulated — ideal for exploring or taking long sunset strolls.

INFORMATION: About 40 mins south of Raglan on sealed and unsealed winding roads. Follow Whaanga Road off Wainui Road.

image © Ken Hansen

RAGLAN

TE ARA KĀKĀRIKI MTB PARK

Tear along mountain bike trails overlooking the west coast with views across Whāingaroa/Raglan Harbour to the laid-back coastal township of Raglan.

Beneath sprawling stands of coastal pine forest, more than 5 kilometres of winding trails offer family-friendly adventures through to gnarly outings for experienced riders. Built by world-class track builders Empire of Dirt, the connecting trails are surrounded by several historic Māori sites within Wainui Reserve, with plenty of coastal vistas.

From the car park at the end of Riria Kereopa Memorial Drive, walk up the steep path to where the trail officially begins. Be careful in winter, as the track can become slippery. Signage near the entrance provides a park overview.

NON-BIKING ADVENTURES

Kids without wheels can still explore the tree huts and roll around in the pine needles near the main entrance on the right. Avoid walking on bike trails for safety reasons.

RAGLAN MTB CLUB

Stay updated with all the local happenings by grabbing a $20 annual membership. Open to riders aged over 12 years old of all riding abilities. Once or twice a month, the club holds group rides.

FIND OUT MORE
raglanmtb.com

INFORMATION

FACILITIES: Toilets at nearby Wainamu Beach. The closest food outlets are in Raglan.

TRAIL GRADES: Grade 2 (easy) to Grade 5 (expert).

OPENING HOURS: Riders can access the park 24 hours.

ENTRANCE FEE: It's free to ride, but a donation to the club is appreciated.

ARE E-BIKES ALLOWED? Yes.

ARE DOGS ALLOWED? Yes, as long as they are under control.

IS RUNNING OR WALKING ALLOWED? In the surrounding areas, not on the trails.

LOCATION: Head south from Raglan on Wainui Road for about 4 km. Turn right onto Rīria Kereopa Memorial Drive — parking near the end.

SH31 KĀWHIA ROAD

TE KAURI PARK CIRCUIT WALK

Descend into a forested valley filled with ferns and soaring rimu. A healthy dose of steps make for an energetic outing.

INFORMATION

GRADE: Medium.

ACCESSIBILITY: Well-graded path with lots of steps.

TIME: Allow 1 hour to 80 min (2.5 km) for the loop.

FACILITIES: No toilet on the main loop.

LOCATION: On SH31 (Kāwhia Road), 20 min before Kāwhia.

DOGS: No dogs.

The restoration of this 1100-hectare native bush remnant near Kāwhia was officially launched in 2002, by renowned botanist Dr David Bellamy. Now, more than two decades later, the diverse valley is home to kārearea/New Zealand falcon and kōtare/sacred kingfisher.

From the parking area outside Te Kauri Lodge on Kāwhia Road, walk east for about 150 metres before crossing the road to access Mānuka Track — take care, as cars zoom around the blind corner. The trail descends steeply into the valley before levelling out at the Waikuku Stream swing bridge to follow the Waikuku Track, shaded by towering trees alongside the stream. A 10-minute side track leads to a small picnic and camping area with a long-drop toilet. Look for korimako/bellbird, tūī, kōtare/sacred kingfisher, kererū/New Zealand pigeon, kārearea/New Zealand falcon and ruru/morepork within the treetops.

After the small wooden bridge, follow the Sheep Track signs — this is where it might start to hurt, as

steep steps exit the valley. The last 200 metres along a fenceline provide impressive views of Kāwhia before the trail connects with the road for a final 150-metre-long walk east back to the lodge where you started.

JUNATS

Hamilton Junior Naturalist Club (Junats) is a club for kids who are enthusiastic about the outdoors and natural history. Members famously discovered a giant penguin fossil near Kāwhia which may be up to 35 million years old. The group regularly hosts camps at its Te Kauri Lodge.

KĀWHIA

TE PUIA SPRINGS

Wallow in a soothing hot-water oasis while avoiding the crowds on a secluded black-sand beach beside the rugged Tasman Sea.

INFORMATION

GRADE: Easy.

ACCESSIBILITY: Short walk over dunes. No lifeguards. Black sand is HOT in summer.

TIME: Allow 1 hour return.

FACILITIES: Toilets near the car park.

LOCATION: From Kāwhia, drive to the end of Te Puia Road (occasionally signposted as Ocean Beach Road).

DOGS: Dogs on leads.

These natural springs near Kāwhia on the West Coast don't draw crowds like Hot Water Beach on the Coromandel Peninsula, so you'll likely be bathing solo.

For two hours on either side of low tide, the vast beach will delight kids, who can roll down the dunes, covering themselves in sand, before jumping into a toasty warm puddle.

Follow the path over the dunes to a seam of hot water on the beach at about 'two o'clock' when viewed from the dunes, or wander around the low-tide mark, digging toes in to feel the warmth of the springs bubbling to the surface.

The sand is quite firm, and deep pools are difficult to dig even with spades. But you can make them large enough to lay in and watch the wild sea.

Avoid rogue waves submerging pools with chilly water by visiting when the tide is retreating.

BLACK SANDS

The black sands on the west coast beaches are rich in iron content from volcanic activity about 2.5 million years ago.

Over time the ocean currents have swept these sands north from near Taranaki and deposited them along the coastline.

The iron-sand deposit at Tahāroa, south of Kāwhia Harbour, is the largest in New Zealand, with an estimated reserve of 300 million tonnes.

Mined sand is used to make steel.

PIOPIO

WAITANGURU FALLS WALK

A leisurely wander through a moss-draped forest leads to a misty waterfall, tumbling 15 metres into a forest-clad plunge pool.

Despite being a mini-adventure, this walk ticks off some picturesque highlights, including a pretty waterfall and hundreds of purple-red parataniwha plants blanketing damp streambeds and gullies.

Surrounded by rugged limestone valley walls and green valley pastures — laden with bouncy lambs during spring — the falls are a worthy detour while travelling in the area.

DENIZE BLUFFS

These 90-metre-high and nearly 2-kilometre-long bluffs are where Sir Peter Jackson filmed scenes for *The Hobbit: An Unexpected Journey,* including Trollshaws Forest and where Gandalf bestowed the sword 'Sting' upon Bilbo. Although they are visible from the road through Mangaotaki Valley, these bluffs can only be accessed through local tour operators for selfies and re-enactments.

INFORMATION

GRADE: Easy.

ACCESSIBILITY: Well-graded path with steps.

TIME: Allow 20 min (400 m) return.

FACILITIES: No toilets.

LOCATION: 19 km from Piopio on Mangaotaki Road.

DOGS: No dogs.

MANGAOTAKI WALK

For an old-school outing, tackle this undulating trail with its jumble of roots past huge boulders draped in epiphytes. Despite not being the most well-maintained trail, it's a fun, rustic, kid-friendly outing. Dozens of plant and tree identification labels add interest, and a small clearing provides views of rugged limestone bluffs.

Allow 40 min (800 m) for the loop. About 8 km along Mangaotaki Road from Piopio. No dogs.

SH4 TE KŪITI

OMARU FALLS WALK

After heavy rain, this waterfall delivers an impressive frothy display while plunging 45 metres off an escarpment surrounded by native bush and farmland.

INFORMATION

GRADE: Easy.

ACCESSIBILITY: Dirt path, steps and pasture.

TIME: Allow 1 hour return.

FACILITIES: No toilets.

LOCATION: 500 metres along Omaru Road, 19 km from SH4/SH3 junction.

DOGS: No dogs.

From the car park, clamber over a stile onto a short farmland section before the trail enters native forest filled with ferns and young rimu. Follow alongside the meandering stream to the wobbly little suspension bridge, with another dose of farmland on the other side — keep an eye out for the orange markers.

Follow alongside the broad river which sweeps across shallow rapids before plunging off the waterfall. Glimpses of the rapids can be spied through the shrubby landscape — there are a handful of grassy viewing spots beside the rapids for riverside picnics.

The final stretch leads to a wooden viewing platform looking across to the waterfall, with excellent top-to-bottom views of the falls and surrounding countryside.

During winter, the streamside path can become boggy, so prepare for muddy shoes and allow extra time to tackle the conditions.

TOUTOUWAI
NORTH ISLAND ROBIN

This gangly, long-legged native bird often forages on the forest floor, looking for critters to munch. They are sometimes spotted following behind hikers, pecking in their footsteps, and occasionally will flit within a metre of people or perch on a still boot. Bachelors are known for their tuneful warbling, which often lasts a few minutes. North Island robins live mainly between Taranaki and the Bay of Plenty. Nesting begins in September, with males delivering food two to three times per hour while the female is sitting on the eggs.

WAITOMO

RUAKURI WALK

This narrow karst gorge draped in native ferns and dewy moss has all the highlights expected from a trip to Waitomo, with a superb display of glowworms appearing at dusk.

The gloomy Ruakuri Natural Tunnel cavern is a highlight of this walk, with its high ceiling echoing sounds from the roaring Waitomo Stream far below. Bring a torch to see stalactites and stalagmites and navigate the slippery steps.

Explore low limestone arches and cliffside boardwalks on a series of loops leading to the tunnel. Before the walk levels out on its return to the car park, a narrow wooden staircase plummets into the forest canopy before disappearing into a cliff where dinosaur-shaped rock formations lurk.

Along the way, listen for kererū/native wood pigeon crashing through the treetops, or tūī, pīwakawaka/fantail and tauhou/silvereye chattering in the canopy.

It's an accessible loop for children, although steep path-side ledges mean toddlers could be safer tucked in a backpack.

TITIWAI GLOWWORMS

If loitering as dusk darkens the landscape, look for the thousands of twinkling titiwai/glowworms near the bridge and forest stream. But as pretty as they are when shrouded in darkness, the misnamed glowworms are actually sluggish-looking fungus gnat larvae. They lure insects to their sticky, silky strands by combining a heady mixture of oxygen, chemicals and enzymes to emit an alluring blue-green glow. Best not spoil the mystique by shining a torch on them!

INFORMATION

GRADE: Easy/Medium.

ACCESSIBILITY: Walking only, due to steep steps, dirt paths and boardwalks. However, turn right at the first junction for a 10-minute buggy-friendly option to the bridge and glowworms.

TIME: Allow 45 min to 1 hour (1 km) for the loop.

FACILITIES: Toilet near the car park.

LOCATION: Drive west from Waitomo and turn left at the roundabout onto Tumutumu Road. The car park is about 2 km further along on the right.

DOGS: No dogs.

WAITOMO

PIRIPIRI CAVE WALK

Explore a dark, slightly spooky cave as gusts of cold wind, emerging from deep underground, whip past the viewing platform.

It's a leisurely walk through native bush to the cave. After a decent dousing of rain, it's like exploring a tropical rainforest trail lined with abundant, bright-green undergrowth with dense, towering tree canopies overhead.

The cave entrance appears after a sharp bend — look for the seat wedged between limestone outcrops. Without a torch, it's tricky to see anything beyond the pitch-black entrance and steps into the cave, where the temperature drops rapidly. Your eyes will slowly adjust in a few minutes.

The cave was originally part of a reef system formed in shallow, warm waters before tectonic uplift raised vast areas of porous limestone. Groundwater erosion then created the underground network of caves.

This short, fun little family adventure is worth ticking off while visiting nearby Marokopa Falls (p68).

INFORMATION

GRADE: Easy.

ACCESSIBILITY: Well-graded paths and steps. Slippery inside the cave.

TIME: Allow 15 min (300 m) return.

FACILITIES: None.

LOCATION: 29 km west of Waitomo on Te Anga Road.

DOGS: No dogs.

WAITOMO

MAROKOPA FALLS

Plunging 35 metres off a jagged lip of greywacke, this waterfall is often shrouded in dazzling rainbows, making it one of the nation's most photographed falls.

From the car park, established tawa and nīkau forest shade the short trail leading to an impressively wizened tree, looming large. Seats beneath the gnarly giant provide 'forest bathing' opportunities for folks taking a breather. Peek behind the tree to see slabs of vertical tree buttresses.

Firmly on the tourist circuit, this well-visited waterfall appeals due to quick accessibility and the picturesque, fan-shaped cascades as the Marokopa River dramatically drops off an escarpment. On windy days, prepare for a soaking as the falls' spray is whipped into a frenzy and deposited on camera-touting visitors. It's worth bringing a lens-cloth to mop away any stray droplets.

The well-graded path lined with parataniwha includes steps and is unsuitable for buggies and wheelchairs.

INFORMATION

GRADE: Easy.

ACCESSIBILITY: Mixture of well-graded paths and steps.

TIME: Allow 20 min (600 m) return.

FACILITIES: None.

LOCATION: 31 km west of Waitomo Village on Te Anga Road.

DOGS: No dogs.

PARATANIWHA

This toothy-leaved member of the nettle family is found naturally only in the North Island, as far south as the Tararua Range.

It grows to about 1 metre high, and its rough leaves are bronze, green and purple. It likes shady, damp areas in the forest and establishes large colonies similar to those beside the Marokopa Falls trail.

Its Māori name roughly translates to 'home of the taniwha'.

WAITOMO

OPAPAKA PĀ WALK

On fine days, this lofty vantage point, with its well-preserved pā remnants, offers sweeping views across farmland scattered with jagged limestone outcrops.

A steady climb through native forest culminates at the breezy peak of this former pā, providing an interesting insight into its tribal history. On the final push to the grassy summit, wind-beaten trees arch across the trail, trunks bent from years of battling solid winds whipping through the valley.

It's obvious why Ngāti Hia occupied this formidable site during times of trouble in the late 1700s. Steep slopes acted as a natural defence against raiding war parties. Still visible are defensive ditches and where wooden palisades once surrounded important living areas. And, on the slopes, the depressions were food storage pits, which would have been covered by timber and earth roofs to protect kūmara and other tubers during winter.

Although it's a solid climb to the pā site, with a healthy dose of stairs, children can conquer this short walk. Plenty of plant identification labels help keep flora boffins motivated on the hike.

INFORMATION

GRADE: Easy/Medium.

ACCESSIBILITY: Well-graded dirt path and steps.

TIME: Allow 1 hour (about 2 km) return.

FACILITIES: No toilets.

LOCATION: About 6.5 km along Waitomo Caves Road from SH3.

DOGS: No dogs.

MĀORI HISTORY

A battle between Ngāti Hia and a war party led by Tāne Tinorau, chief of Kāwhia, erupted at this summit. After the fighting, Tinorau lay down his dog-skin cloak as a sign of peace and the area became known as Te Horahanga o te Kahu o Tāne Tinorau, the place where Tāne Tinorau spread out his garment.

JOURNEY ALONG THE RAILS

HAURAKI RAIL TRAIL

Replacing trains chugging along New Zealand's oldest railway corridor are two-wheel enthusiasts pedalling the Hauraki Rail Trail, one of the country's easiest cycle trails. Five sections connect the shell-littered coastline of Tīkapa Moana/Firth of Thames, historic mineral pools and historic mining and spa towns to the rural township of Matamata. The mainly flat, nearly 200-kilometre-long trail is a Grade 1 cycle trail, suitable for most fitness and skill levels. For current trail conditions and trail maps, visit haurakirailtrail.co.nz.

SECTION A | KAIAUA TO THAMES

Beginning in the seaside village of Kaiaua, pedal alongside Tīkapa Moana/ Firth of Thames past wetlands, farmland and views across the harbour to the Coromandel Peninsula. Don't miss calling into the Pūkorokoro Miranda Shorebird Centre (p10) to learn more about the remarkable annual migration of kuaka/bar-tailed godwits. After the Kopu Bridge, the trail turns north to reach the former gold-mining township of Thames.

53 km one way. Grade 1 (easiest). Allow 5 to 6 hours one way.

SECTION B | THAMES TO PAEROA

From Thames, follow the old railway south out of town past farmland, with views of the Hauraki Plains and forested Kaimai Range. There are glimpses of the Waihou River, possibly some anglers, the occasional seal and lots of īnanga/whitebait. Finish a day in the saddle with a selfie beside the giant L&P bottle. There is an optional riverboat cruise from the Historical Maritime Park into Paeroa.

32 km one way. Grade 1 (easiest). Allow 3 to 4 hours one way.

SECTION D | PAEROA TO TE AROHA

Beginning near the Paeroa floodgates, the flat trail winds through the alluvial Hauraki Plains on wide cycleways and along brief road sections while skirting the fringes of the Kaimai Mamaku Conservation Park. The mighty maunga Te Aroha ('Mountain of Love') dominates the eastern skyline. Pedal-weary legs will appreciate a post-adventure dip into the soothing, silky mineral pools at the Edwardian domain.

23 km one way. Grade 1 (easiest). Allow 2 to 3 hours one way.

SECTION E | TE AROHA TO MATAMATA

Leaving Te Aroha Domain, cycle south past horse studs, views of the North Island's tallest waterfall, Wairere Falls, and the bush-clad Kaimai Range with its hidden relics of the 1880s gold-rush days. Cross the East Coast Main Trunk Line and take a break at the Firth Tower to explore the reserve's tower, jail and settler cottage. The final long, straight section of trail ends in Matamata at the Hobbiton-themed information centre.

34 km one way. Grade 1 (easiest). Allow 2 to 4 hours one way.

SECTION C

PAEROA TO WAIHI

This crowd-pleasing section of the Hauraki Rail Trail is an out-and-back detour jam-packed with historic mining and railway relics. A spooky railway tunnel, dramatic gorge and historic cyanide tanks will tempt everyone to keep pedalling happily along.

The 24-kilometre-long trail officially begins on Rotokohu Road in Paeroa and ends at the Goldfields Railway Station in Waihi. Following rural roads from Paeroa, there's a short farmland section before entering the steep-sided Karangahake Gorge.

The trail from Paeroa to Waihi takes about 2 to 3 hours (one way) and is graded easiest (Grade 1). It's an excellent option for older riders wanting some miles in the saddle. But, because most kid-friendly highlights are bunched near the middle, the beginning and end might not engage younger riders.

Trim 6 kilometres by starting beside the Karangahake Hall on Crown Hill Road.

Cross the Ōhinemuri River pedestrian bridge to the gloomy 1100-metre-long rail tunnel, which was once part of the Waikato and Bay of Plenty rail network, when gold fever ran rampant through the gorge. Chilled air escaping from the tunnel blasts bikers entering the arched engineering feat, and dim lights illuminate the way. Keep an eye on kids scooting ahead, as bikers rapidly appear from both ends.

The trail follows the Ōhinemuri River to the remnant of the vast Victoria Battery, which closed in 1952 — don't miss taking a quick detour to the picturesque Owharoa Falls (p72). The battery crushed ore from Martha Mine in Waihi before gold was extracted from the ore using a potassium cyanide solution. Kids will love poking around in the Roman-style ruins despite its grim-sounding past.

HAURAKI RAIL TRAIL HIGHLIGHTS

- Jump on a vintage train from Waikino to Waihi, then peer into the immense Martha Mine.
- Selfie at the famous L&P bottle.
- Soothe away aches in Te Aroha's mineral pools.
- Pedal through the dramatic, bush-clad Karangahake Gorge.

IMPORTANT

1. Plan your route: The trail is well signposted, but maps are handy.

2. Tell someone about your plans. Avoid riding alone and take a mobile phone.

3. Be aware of the weather: Always take a rain jacket and warm clothes.

4. Know your limits: ride within your physical limits and ability.

5. Take sufficient supplies, including a bike-repair kit, for the worst-case scenario, and plenty of water.

SAFETY TIPS

These simple tips help bikers stay safe while cycling the trail: Be Seen, Be Aware, Be Predictable, Be Confident, Be Safe, Be Patient and Be Prepared.

SECTION C
SHORT ADVENTURE

For a quick 1-hour adventure, pedal through the dimly lit tunnel, then, at the end, jump off the bikes to explore beneath the Ohinemuri River bridge. Here the kids can have a paddle, enjoy a picnic and soak up the views of the rugged Karangahake Gorge before heading home. Ideal for young bikers.

GRADE: Easiest (Grade 1).

DISTANCE: About 3 km return from Karangahake Hall.

SECTION C
HALF-DAY ADVENTURE

Explore the historic tunnel before following the trail to the imposing Victoria Battery ruins. During weekends and public holidays, volunteers from the Victoria Battery Tramway & Museum Society operate a miniature train on a 2-foot-gauge tramway, host underground tours and open the nearby museum (a small charge applies). Waikino Railway Station is across the footbridge for refuelling with snacks and coffee.

GRADE: Easiest (Grade 1).

DISTANCE: About 14 km return from Karangahake Hall.

FIND OUT MORE
vbts.org.nz

SECTION C
FULL-DAY ADVENTURE

Bike to Waikino Railway Station and jump on a historic tourist train to Waihi. Explore the deep Martha Mine, Waihi Gold Discovery Centre and sample local fare at the cafés. Catch a returning train or add an extra 9 kilometres by biking back to Waikino Railway Station before continuing to Karangahake Hall. Goldfields Railway operates departures during the week and on weekends.

GRADE: Easiest (Grade 1).

DISTANCE: About 14 km return from Karangahake Hall (optional additional 9 km).

FIND OUT MORE
waihirail.co.nz

KARANGAHAKE GORGE
OWHAROA FALLS

This little adventure is a short, 2-minute stroll to a multi-tiered waterfall, making it ideal for youngsters. Don't miss when travelling through Karangahake Gorge! A flat area beside the main 6-metre-high waterfall provides a vantage point from which to admire the cascading falls — ideal for picnics. Although this is a popular swimming spot in summer with locals, keep safety in mind when taking a dip.

INFORMATION

Turn off Karangahake Gorge (SH2) onto Waitawheta Road, Waikino. There is limited parking immediately after the bridge. Suitable for walking only. Dogs on leads.

MORRINSVILLE
MORRINSVILLE RIVER WALK

During summer, when the water is low, clamber over flat rock formations exposed in the stream bed. However, the river turns into an impressive torrent in winter after heavy rain, so it's worth visiting throughout the year.

Shaded by lofty, mature natives, the dirt path passes a large stand of tōtara. An alternative higher trail runs parallel with the main path, often connecting, so perhaps try both — the lower path one way and the upper option when returning.

INFORMATION: Allow 1 to 2 hours (3.6 km) return. Walking only. Dirt paths with steps. Dogs on leads. No facilities.

LOCATION: Plenty of parking at the Morrinsville Recreation Ground entrance on Avenue Road South.

KAIMAI RANGE
MCLAREN FALLS

Explore immense slabs of rock pockmarked with warm pools and trickling waterfalls. Take a dip or wet your toes in the shallow pools of the forest-edged Mangakarengorengo River — watch for tuna/eels slithering by! The river is part of the Kaimai Power Scheme, which releases water year-round.

Find a perch on the vast rocky ledges, grab something to eat and survey the activity.

During winter, the waterfall puts on an impressive show, with countless cascading drops.

INFORMATION: Limited parking is available beside the waterfall. No facilities. Always read the safety signs beside the bridge for water-release dates.

LOCATION: Turn off SH29 onto McLaren Falls Road.

KAIMAI RANGE
WATERFALL TRACK

Visit McLaren Falls Park for an easy streamside trail through native bush, leading to a vantage point above a pretty waterfall before looping back on the other side of the stream to the car park. At dusk, the damp banks lining the pathway glisten with thousands of white-orbed glowworms. The sprawling park covers 190 hectares beside Lake McLaren, an excellent day-tripping destination for lakeside picnics, kayaking and nature exploring. In autumn, the botanical tree collection has gorgeous vibrant burnt orange and yellow leaves. It's buggy-friendly only on the left-hand side of the stream.

INFORMATION: Allow 20 min return. Check gate closure times on arrival. Café, information centre, electric barbecue, campsites and plenty of toilets. No dogs.

LOCATION: McLaren Falls Park. Turn off SH29 onto McLaren Falls Road on the eastern side of the Kaimai Range and continue to the park's entrance.

TE AROHA | MATAMATA

WAIRERE FALLS TRACK

The beguiling roar of the North Island's highest waterfall echoes down a steep valley past mammoth moss-covered boulders and cascading watering holes.

This walk is not for the faint-hearted, as it can be slippery on the rocks, steps and exposed roots. Allow extra time for kids and enjoy a few snack breaks on the way up.

image © Gary Clare

Pause on the wooden bridges for picturesque views of the bush-shrouded Wairere Stream and popular summer-dipping watering holes. Then conquer the near-vertical set of stairs to emerge into the upper gorge, lined with groves of nīkau and pūriri before views appear of the tiered waterfall.

From the lookout, take a breather and watch the 153-metre-high waterfall. It's impressive at all times, but on windy days the falls are blown apart like delicate lace or entirely upwards. The falls plummet off a steep escarpment created by uplift caused by the Ōkauia fault.

After rain, small waterfalls drip from moss-covered rock walls beside the trail. And in spring, look for the apricot-coloured, trumpet-shaped flowers of the native taurepo plant, which are well suited to the long, tapered beaks of honeyeaters such as hihi/stitchbird and tīeke/saddleback.

UPPER LOOKOUT

For a longer adventure, continue to the upper viewpoint with its expanse of exposed rocks and grand views spanning the Waikato Basin. Best attempted by the fit and keen, as it will add another 60 to 90 minutes return to the lower lookout. There's a gut-busting section to navigate shortly after leaving the lower lookout, but it levels out closer to the top, where there's a pretty trail through native forest. Midsummer, the exposed rocks are fun to clamber over. Be extremely careful near the edge of the falls.

WAIKATO WETLANDS

Up until the early 1800s, the Waikato Basin was a vast wetland wonderland. Peat lakes and wetlands covered the landscape with thriving populations of native birds and various critters, shaded in places by towering stands of kahikatea. Yet today, less than a quarter of this flourishing ecosystem remains after vast swathes were drained for farmland.

Following European settlement, thousands of hectares of Waikato wetlands were converted to pasture. But although the landscape has dramatically changed, Waikato still holds some of New Zealand's most significant wetlands.

There are two primary varieties: low-nutrient wetlands (bogs) and highly fertile wetlands (swamps). No two wetlands are precisely alike; each has diverse plants and animals, and local conditions dictate which plants and animals thrive where. And, as environmental conditions change, so does wetland diversity. Many wetland plants and animals face extinction due to habitat loss and wetlands becoming fragmented. Human activity near wetlands can also have a negative impact, especially when the water table drops or if nutrients in the soil and water increase.

Explore notable wetland remnants at Lake Kainui (p18), Waihora Lagoon (p177), Howarth Memorial Wetland (top picture and p78), Lake Rotopiko (p43) and Yarndley's Bush (p40).

INFORMATION

GRADE: Medium/Hard.

ACCESSIBILITY: Boardwalks, dirt paths with rocks, roots and uneven steps.

TIME: Allow 45 min one way to the lower lookout.

FACILITIES: Toilet near the car park.

LOCATION: 15 min from Matamata or 20 min south of Te Aroha on Goodwin Road off Old Te Aroha Road.

DOGS: No dogs.

SAVE OUR KAURI FORESTS

They are dying from kauri dieback disease

It spreads by soil movement
ACT NOW to help stop it

ALWAYS

1. SCRUB YOUR GEAR
Remove soil before AND after forest visits – scrub your shoes, tyres and equipment

2. STAY ON THE TRACK
AND off kauri roots

www.kauridieback.co.nz

TĀNGATA WHENUA | MINISTRY FOR PRIMARY INDUSTRIES | DEPARTMENT OF CONSERVATION | NORTHLAND REGIONAL COUNCIL | AUCKLAND COUNCIL | WAIKATO REGIONAL COUNCIL | BAY OF PLENTY REGIONAL COUNCIL

KD012 March 2019

KO TĀTOU THIS IS US

BIOSECURITY 2025

NATIVE TREES

TRUNKS AND BARKS

Sometimes you can't see the tops of towering trees poking through the forest canopy. So instead of getting a kink in your neck, here are a few different trunks and bark patterns to look out for – everything from flaky and stringy, to trunks that look like someone has dented them with a hammer!

1

2

3

4

5

6

1. TŌTARA

The trunk has thick, stringy, reddish-grey bark that peels off in long strips.

2. KAURI

The trunk looks like it has hammer marks on it, and leaks gum.

3. RIMU

The drooping, flaky bark has a deep red colour.

4. NĪKAU PALM

The trunk has circular grey-green scars where fronds have fallen off.

5. PONGA | SILVER FERN

White undersides on the fronds, and sometimes dead frond 'skirts' around the upper trunk.

6. PŌHUTUKAWA

Usually grows as a multi-trunked spreading tree. The bark is rough and stringy.

TE AROHA

HOWARTH MEMORIAL WETLAND

Budding bird enthusiasts will be quivering through their binoculars at this regenerating wetland, a former swampy dumping ground for rubbish. After its transformation into a wildlife refuge, matuku moana/white-faced heron, tētē moroiti/grey teal and kawau pū/black shag have all been spotted loitering within the wetland.

Mount Te Aroha provides an imposing backdrop for the wide, mainly flat path looping around the wetland. Peer into the wetland's murky depths, looking for water-dwelling critters from the wooden viewing platform.

If bikes are onboard, the nearby BMX track at the end of Spur Street should burn off some extra energy (although there is no biking around the wetlands).

INFORMATION: Allow 1 hour (about 3 km) to complete the loop. Buggy-friendly aside from a few small rooty sections, and the family pooch is welcome. No bikes.

LOCATION: Plenty of parking on Spur Street.

TE AROHA

UPPER AND LOWER DOMAIN WALKS

Combine both walks for a quick dose of nature in the foothills of Mount Te Aroha before exploring the spa town and nearby playground.

Beginning behind the mineral spas at Te Aroha Domain, stroll along the loop winding past nīkau, native ferns, an old water reservoir and the perky Mōkena Geyser (p79). Glimpses across Te Aroha township appear between trees, and kids can clamber through a narrow earth cutting. At night bring a torch to discover glowworms clinging to damp forest banks.

INFORMATION: Allow 30 min (about 1.5 km) return to complete both walks. The Lower Walk is suitable for buggies as an out-and-back, or exit onto the grassy domain. The Upper Walk is walking only. Dogs on leads. Toilets, cafés, thermal pools and playground.

LOCATION: Limited parking within Te Aroha Domain. Plenty of parking on nearby Boundary Road.

TE AROHA

TŪĪ DOMAIN TRACK

Not too long, not too short; this family-sized adventure begins beside Mōkena Geyser before sidling around the base of Mount Te Aroha to a rocky outcrop and the picturesque Tutumangaeo Falls.

The dirt track leads past overgrown historical relics hidden in the shrubbery before reaching Noel's Lookout for views towards the Hapuakohe Range. Then, dip down along a rocky ridge to the base of Tutumangaeo Falls and take a breather while the kids paddle and look for kōura/freshwater crayfish.

Return the same way or cross the wooden plank for a slightly more adventurous outing navigating the winding, often unmarked trails back to Te Aroha Domain.

INFORMATION: Allow 1 hour return. Walking only. Dogs on leads.

LOCATION: Limited parking within Te Aroha Domain. Plenty of parking on nearby Boundary Road.

TE AROHA

WHAKAPIPI LOOKOUT

If the troops aren't ready to conquer Mount Te Aroha, the highest point of the Kaimai Mamaku Conservation Park, this scenic alternative still has big views from its lower vantage point.

INFORMATION

GRADE: Medium.

ACCESSIBILITY: Dirt paths, sometimes rooty, with steps.

TIME: Allow 45 min one way to the lookout.

FACILITIES: Plenty of snacks, ice-cream shops, cafés, an information centre and toilets in Te Aroha.

LOCATION: The trailhead begins beside Mōkena Geyser. Limited parking within Te Aroha Domain. Plenty of parking nearby on Boundary Road.

DOGS: Dogs on leads.

The well-formed trail ascends quickly, zigzagging past introduced pines, native trees and swathes of parataniwha (p68) before reaching the lookout at about 350 metres above sea level. There's seating with views across wetlands and rural landscapes to extinct volcanoes on the horizon, and the Waihou River snaking past the bird-refuge Howarth Memorial Wetland on the outskirts of Te Aroha (p78).

It's a popular walk with locals, despite being a steady climb — snacks and drinks will help flagging enthusiasm levels. On hot days, stiff breezes often whip through the trees to cool off hikers, but prepare for slippery trails after rain.

From the lookout, return down the same way unless wanting to unintentionally summit Te Aroha a few hours later.

MOUNT TE AROHA

Allow another couple of hours from the lookout to reach the summit of Mount Te Aroha for 360-degree views of both sides of the Kaimai Range.

MŌKENA GEYSER

In Te Aroha Domain, the world's only known hot soda-water geyser erupts in a frothy frenzy every 40 minutes.

Clear, clean water spurts nearly 3 metres into the air behind the mineral spa building, coming from about 70 metres underground. The bore currently produces 28,000 litres of water daily at a temperature between 75 and 85°C, which is used in the nearby pools.

The geyser is named after Māori chief Mōkena Te Hau, who once owned the domain land. His memorial cairn is next to the gazebo.

TE AROHA

BUTLERS INCLINE LOW-LEVEL LOOP

This eye-wateringly steep mining incline delivers a merciless outing on the pine-clad slopes of Waiorongomai Valley, disappearing skyward for 400 metres at a vertigo-inducing 25-degree angle.

There's only a distant speck of sunshine to clamber towards on this impressive engineering relic, abandoned in the early 1900s when impenetrable rock thwarted miners' efforts to extract riches from the valley's gold-bearing reefs.

Butlers Incline was built as one of three self-acting inclines along the 3.7-kilometre Piako County Tramway, used to transport ore to nearby batteries for processing.

Explore this adventure a couple of ways, easy or challenging. Both begin from the car park, where the well-graded path climbs through the former lower Waiorongomai gold fields. Native trees and ferns cover the steep valley sides, with pesky radiata pine poking through the canopy. Seeds from this pest tree notoriously follow miners worldwide on boots and gear.

A few shallow streams can easily be navigated by hopping over the rocks before the trail passes several historical sites, including tunnels used by miners and horses to protect them from an aerial ropeway operating above.

At the base of the incline, marvel at how the ore was carted down the hillside while having a well-earned snack, before walking back to the car park along the old railway. Some original parts are still intact.

On the way out, Fern Spur Incline — although not as impressive as Butlers Incline — has countryside views and a Jenga-styled pile of railway sleepers.

HARDER OPTION

Alternatively, climb to the top of the incline, which makes it a nearly 9-kilometre-long return trip from the car park. Check doc.govt.nz for the latest track conditions before attempting. This option suits fit older kids and those who don't mind burning quads.

TE AROHA DOMAIN

GOLD FEVER TO SPAS

For more than a century, it's been boom or bust at Te Aroha. But situated beneath the highest peak on the Kaimai Range, the plucky township has weathered its fair share of chequered fortunes.

Long gone are the old-timer gold prospectors and ailing Victorians seeking the rejuvenating waters of the former spa town, replaced by weekend-visiting outdoorsy families.

Gold-bearing quartz was discovered by prospector Hōne Werahiko near Bald Spur in 1880, and thousands of prospectors rapidly descended on the town.

But when harsh conditions and unyielding rock sent thousands of gold prospectors packing only months after their arrival, enterprising townsfolk began touting an alluring tourist drawcard, even before the dust from the miners' departure had settled.

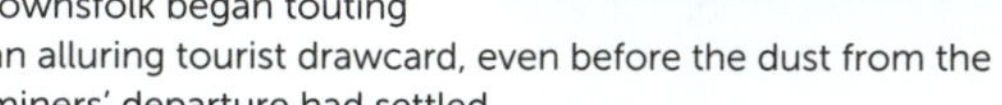

Silky, piping-hot mineral water coming out of the ground had the infirm flocking to the town, where 'taking the waters' was said to cure many ailments. But with medical advances, bathing became more recreational, and the geothermal marvels of Rotorua lured many tourists away.

Today, follow in the prospectors' footsteps along well-travelled adventures hidden in the hills while keeping an eye out for flecks of gold in the mountain streams.

Don't miss visiting the quaint Edwardian Te Aroha Domain with its café, public swimming pool, playground, picnic areas and private mineral pools. The community has fiercely protected the character of the domain and although many original buildings were lost, it remains one of the most intact Edwardian-era domains in New Zealand.

INFORMATION

GRADE: Easy or Hard.

ACCESSIBILITY: Dirt paths and shallow stream crossings.

TIME: Allow 2 hours (5.5 km) return for the Low-Level Loop.

FACILITIES: Rustic toilet a few minutes along the trail.

LOCATION: Parking at the end of Waiorongomai Loop Road near Te Aroha.

DOGS: No dogs.

KARANGAHAKE GORGE

RAIL TUNNEL LOOP

Explore a historic railway tunnel carved into a mountainside more than 100 years ago before sidling alongside dramatic cliffs and the beautiful Ōhinemuri River.

After crossing the footbridge beside Karangahake Hall, plunge yourself into the tunnel's murky darkness, stretching 1.1 kilometres towards a tiny pinprick of light in the distance. Dim lighting illuminates the damp, dripping walls and dirt paths, making navigating relatively easy. But torches are handy, and kids can create cool shadows along the way.

The tunnel was once part of the main line between Waikato and the Bay of Plenty, which opened in 1905 to support the region's gold-mining endeavours. However, it closed when the Kaimai Tunnel opened in 1978.

Emerge into the blinding light and turn right to follow the path hugging the Ōhinemuri River. Some parts of the narrow path are precariously close to the river, so keep an eye on little ones, but it's such a cool adventure within a deep gorge with towering trees above.

The final stretch along a wide path surrounded by regenerating forest passes the ruins of the once imposing Crown Battery, which dominated the gorge, beside the Karangahake Hall car park. Here, in the pursuit of gold, kauri forests were logged, dams built and quartz reefs extracted from deep underground. Stamper batteries crushed quartz before cyanide was used to extract gold from the ore.

Bikes are allowed through the tunnel on the Hauraki Rail Trail (p70) but not on the return track beside the Ōhinemuri River.

The tunnel is suitable for buggies, but not advisable beside the river due to very narrow paths.

MĀORI HISTORY

Ōhinemuri River was an important transport route for Māori between the Hauraki Plains and the Bay of Plenty, and many pā and wharves were built beside the river.

SPOT THE DIFFERENCE

GECKO OR SKINK?

New Zealand has more than 100 species of geckos and skinks which are not found anywhere else. Here are some of their differences so you can tell them apart.

- Geckos have loose, velvety skin that looks one size too large. Skinks are smooth-skinned, sleek and shiny, with small legs.
- Geckos' eyes are large, and they can't blink. They have to clean their eyes with their tongue! Skinks blink.
- When geckos shed their skin it comes off in one go, or in large pieces. Skinks rub their skin off in small patches.
- Geckos have big, round toes with pads covered in microscopic hairs. These hairs give them the ability to climb, even upside down on a ceiling. Skinks have very slender toes and don't have the same toe pads.
- Geckos can vocalise. Many of our species make a chirping sound.

Top: Coromandel striped gecko (image © Thomas David Miles ZOOM-OLOGY.com). Above: Common skink. Text © Waikato Regional Council.

INFORMATION

GRADE: Easy.

ACCESSIBILITY: Well-graded dirt and concrete paths, narrow at times. Dim lighting in the tunnel.

TIME: Allow 90 min (2.5 km) for the loop.

FACILITIES: Toilets beside the car park.

LOCATION: Parking beside Karangahake Hall on Crown Hill Road (off SH2) between Paeroa and Waihi.

DOGS: No dogs.

KARANGAHAKE GORGE
CROWN TRACK

From Dickey Flat campsite, stroll through the spindly native forest before crossing the Waitawheta River and following alongside the rock-strewn waters until reaching a dark, narrow tunnel. This rugged 200-metre-long tunnel has jagged, rocky outcrops — bring a torch to navigate the uneven surface.

After the tunnel, a waterfall ploughs through a hole in a cliff beside an idyllic summer swimming hole. Bring some snacks and laze on the riverbank. During the gold rush, the river powered stamping batteries near where it merged with the Ōhinemuri River. Near its headwaters, tuna/eels, banded kōkopu, brown trout and kōura/freshwater crayfish have been spotted.

INFORMATION: Allow 20 min one way from the campsite. Toilets at the campsite. Dogs on leads.

LOCATION: Dickey Flat Road off SH2, Waikino.

KARANGAHAKE GORGE
KARANGAHAKE WINDOWS WALK

Peer through 'windows' carved into historic mining tunnels high above a roaring river. From the car park, cross the suspension bridges over the Ōhinemuri and Waitawheta Rivers before climbing the stairs and a quick detour to the deep ore-roasting kilns before following the tramline as it passes the hulking concrete ruins of the Talisman Battery. The trail disappears into a mining tunnel with holes carved into the rock faces, creating pockets of light and giving lofty views of the gorge.

INFORMATION: At the time of writing, this walk was closed due to rock instability but is expected to reopen after remedial works. For the latest trail information and an activity map, visit doc.govt.nz.

LOCATION: Karangahake Domain car park off SH2 between Paeroa and Waihi.

KAIMAI MAMAKU RANGE
DALY'S CLEARING HUT

For families wanting an accessible backcountry experience, this short hike provides a kid-friendly overnight adventure. Follow a historic tramline through Waitawheta Valley on a relatively flat trail before detouring towards the Kaimai Mamaku Range on a narrower path that climbs steadily to the brightly coloured hut. Choose from 16 bunks beside the separate dining and accommodation spaces, or pitch a tent on the clearing outside and listen to nocturnal animals rustling in the treetops. If things go pear-shaped, being reasonably close to the car provides a quick escape to civilisation.

INFORMATION: Buy hut tickets from doc.govt.nz. No bookings are required. Allow 90 to 150 min one way. Basic toilet facilities and water (needs to be boiled). No gas or cooking facilities. No dogs.

LOCATION: Parking at the end of Franklin Road off Waitawheta Road near Waikino (SH2).

TĪRAU | PUTĀRURU

TE WAIHOU WALKWAY

Discover sparkling, emerald-coloured springs and the source of some of the world's purest water along a family-friendly trail.

Follow a short, flat trail beside the spring-fed Waihou River — filled with lush, flowing green reeds and tumbling white pebbles — before reaching the blue-green springs.

Emerging from deep underground after a 50- to 100-year journey from the Mamaku Plateau, the pure water supplies about 70 per cent of New Zealand's bottled water and maintains a constant 11°C temperature year-round.

Viewing platforms protect the fragile ecology of the springs; as inviting as it looks, swimming is not permitted. Spread a picnic blanket beneath shady trees lining the river and watch trout swimming lazily in the clear water. The only downside to this popular adventure is the crowds mid-summer.

LONGER OPTION

A longer walk begins from Whites Road (SH28), along an easy-going trail past farmland, wetlands, waterfalls, native bush and the Waihou River. Allow between 2 to 3 hours (9 km) return.

INFORMATION

GRADE: Easy.

ACCESSIBILITY: Well-graded dirt paths and boardwalk.

TIME: Allow 30 min return from Leslie Road entrance.

FACILITIES: Toilets available.

LOCATION: Leslie Road, off SH28, Putāruru.

DOGS: No dogs.

TOETOE

These giant grasses are an iconic part of the landscape, with large light golden-yellow flower plumes draping off tall stems.

But toetoe are often confused with the invasive pampas weed (right).

The easiest way to distinguish between the two is by looking at the flower head; pampas have dense, fluffy flower heads like a feather duster, while toetoe (left) have drooping flower heads. The general rule of thumb is that toetoe flowers before Christmas, while pampas flowers afterwards.

Both have the unfortunate nickname of cutty grass – something off-piste adventurers try to avoid!

PEDAL ALONGSIDE A MIGHTY RIVER

WAIKATO RIVER TRAILS

The Waikato River Trails follow New Zealand's longest river, with bikers pedalling past native forests, historic landmarks, intriguing rock and geological formations, and winding boardwalks over thriving wetlands. This 104-kilometre-long trail is suitable for mountain biking, walking and running, and provides access to areas previously seen by only a few. The five sections are rideable all year round. Find out more at waikatorivertrails.co.nz.

KARĀPIRO TRAIL

An easy roadside section leaves Pokaiwhenua Bridge car park alongside Horahora Road before following the Waikato River beneath native forest and over wetlands on a 500-metre-long boardwalk. Refuel with snacks at Arapuni Village before visiting the Arapuni suspension bridge.

INFORMATION: Grade 3 (intermediate). Parking at either end. 11.5 km. Toilets available.

ARAPUNI TRAIL

Begin the adventure near the dramatic sandstone cliffs at Waipāpa Power Station and pedal north on this on-road section through farmland, with Maungatautari on the horizon, before arriving at Arapuni Power Station and the nearby nerve-testing suspension bridge (p88).

INFORMATION: Grade 3 (intermediate). Parking at either end. 34.6 km. Toilets available.

WAIPĀPA TRAIL

Pedal from Mangakino Lakefront Reserve to the forest edge and beginning of the trail. Explore the looming remnants of an old concrete plant and dam-viewing platforms. Includes on- and off-road sections before ending at Waipāpa Power Station.

INFORMATION: Grade 4 (advanced). Parking at either end. 19.6 km. Toilets available.

MARAETAI TRAIL

Beginning beside the Whakamaru Dam, the trail descends through farmland and forest to the mid-way 70-metre-long Mangakino suspension bridge. Picturesque vistas of Lake Maraetai lead bikers to the trail end at the Mangakino Lakefront Reserve.

INFORMATION: Grade 3 (intermediate). Parking at either end. 12.3 km. Toilets available.

WHAKAMARU TRAIL

From the water's edge at the Lake Ātiamuri boat ramp, pedal through diverse landscapes, including the dramatic volcanic 'plug' Pōhaturoa, the Ōngāroto Bluffs staircase with its impressive views and boardwalks beside farmland before ending at Whakamaru Dam.

INFORMATION: Grade 3 (intermediate). Parking at either end. 26 km. Toilets available.

KARĀPIRO SECTION
LITTLE WAIPĀ TO ARAPUNI

This shorter option is part of the Karapiro section and is ideal for first-timers looking to sample the Waikato River Trails on a leisurely ride alongside the Waikato River.

INFORMATION

GRADE: Grade 3 (intermediate).

ACCESSIBILITY: Mixture of well-graded gravel, boardwalk and short road sections.

TIME: Allow 30–45 min (6.2 km) one way biking from Little Waipā Reserve to Arapuni village.

FACILITIES: Café, toilets and picnic tables.

LOCATION: Parking at either Little Waipā Reserve or Arapuni village.

DOGS: No dogs.

Although the Karāpiro section 'officially' begins 5 kilometres north of Little Waipā Reserve at the Pokaiwhenua Bridge, starting at Little Waipā Reserve saves a few kilometres to help younger kids last longer on this out-and-back adventure. It offers easy pedalling, with only a few challenging steep parts.

Cycle between farmland and the meandering Waikato River from the reserve to reach the impressive 500-metre-long Huihuitaha Wetland boardwalk, winding through a regenerating wetland. Keep an eye out for kōtare/sacred kingfisher and pīwakawaka/ fantails. Pack snacks for a mid-way refuelling stop at the picnic tables.

Before Arapuni village, navigate a short road section on the quiet Powerhouse Road before dipping under the shady canopy of lofty trees for the final cycle into the village.

After enjoying a picnic or a bite to eat at the café, test everyone's nerves while crossing the nearby mammoth suspension bridge dangling over the gorge (p88). After the bridge, bike to the lower bridge and reconnect with Powerhouse Road, leading to the trail again.

ARAPUNI

ARAPUNI SUSPENSION BRIDGE

Dangling over the Waikato River, this wobbly suspension bridge provides impressive bird's-eye-views of ancient volcanic cliffs and Arapuni Power Station.

From the bridge, kids can peer down at the working hydroelectric station, and the sheer volcanic cliffs downstream on the right, before strolling down to the lower bridge where you can admire the narrow gorge from another angle. Then go back up the hill to connect with the village track on the right. All well signposted.

The bridge is considered a Category II historic place and was completed in 1926 to provide workers living in Arapuni village easy access to the dam's spillway and powerhouse.

INFORMATION: Allow 30 min return. Suitable for walking, buggies and biking. Café, toilets and picnic areas. Dogs on leads.

LOCATION: Parking at Arapuni Village Green, Arapuni Road, Arapuni.

WAOTU | ARAPUNI

JIM BARNETT RESERVE

Sheltered by a small hill from the fiery blast of Taupō erupting, this valley has an ancient forest with numerous trails leading to a 1000-year-old tōtara.

The most accessible trail is the Tāne Track (allow 20 to 30 min return), but for more highlights combine the Tāne Track and Tōtara Track past the wizened ancient tōtara, ending beside a stand of trees with identification signs near the car park.

The well-maintained dirt path has occasional narrow, rooty sections and steps. To successfully navigate the reserve, grab a trail map from the car park or snap a photo of the sign.

INFORMATION: Walking only on the Tōtara Trail. Tāne Trail is suitable for buggies. Allow 1 hour return. Shelter and toilets by the car park. No dogs.

LOCATION: Waotu South Road, Waotu. About 15 min from Arapuni village.

WHAKAMARU

ŌNGĀROTO BLUFFS

Clamber up five flights of steep stairs to a vantage point high above the Waikato River with swoon-worthy views down an often misty valley.

Despite the climb, the views of SH30 snaking its way south past sheer rock faces are worth the effort.

It's part of the Whakamaru section of the Waikato River Trails (p86), but can be done as a quick detour if passing.

INFORMATION: Allow 15 min return. Walking only. No facilities. Dogs on leads.

LOCATION: Roadside parking on SH30 about 4.5 km south of the SH30/SH32 junction. Then it's a further couple of hundred metres walking south to the steps.

TOKOROA

COUGAR MTB PARK

With exceptional flowing trails winding through South Waikato forestry land, this easily accessible park has trails for keen bikers of all abilities.

Purpose-built with 50 kilometres of off-road forest tracks within 68 hectares of pine plantation, this park has grown in popularity with Waikato mountain bikers and those from outside the region looking for quality off-road action.

The park has 35 tracks ranging from easy to expert, catering to beginner bikers and experienced folks in the saddle, with new trails under development. All routes are well signposted, and multiple trail maps are displayed throughout the park, helping keep everyone on track.

WHERE TO START?

For beginners, the Newell Road entrance, about 1.5 kilometres north of the town centre, is near excellent Grade 1 and 2 tracks, including Fred Flintstone (image above) and Yabba Dabba Doo.

The main entrance is off Mossop Road, part of the Tokoroa Memorial Sports Ground south of the Tokoroa CBD on SH1, with a pump and skills tracks for all ages.

TOKOROA MTB CLUB

After forming in the 1990s, the club has created a professional network of trails at Cougar MTB Park. During the school term, the club hosts junior training nights every Wednesday, and runs group rides for all abilities year-round. Annual subscriptions are available for individuals and families. Check out the club's website for more information and trail maps.

FIND OUT MORE
tokoroamountainbikeclub.co.nz

INFORMATION

FACILITIES: At Mossop Road car park, there is a public toilet, a water fountain at the entrance pavilion and a bike-cleaning station at the maintenance sheds. No facilities at Newell Road car park.

TRAIL GRADES: A mix of Grade 2 (easy) to Grade 5 (expert).

OPENING HOURS: Riders can access the park 24 hours.

ENTRANCE FEE: It's free to ride at Cougar Park. The club does encourage users to become members of the Tokoroa MTB Club to help with trail building and maintenance costs.

ARE E-BIKES ALLOWED? Yes.

ARE WALKERS AND DOGS ALLOWED? Walkers with dogs are fine on the entrance track, any climb, and on connecting roads within the park boundaries. However, for safety reasons, walkers and dogs are not allowed on downhill sections.

EXPLORE THE

BAY OF PLENTY

Soak in steamy geothermal pools, hug mighty kauri trees or nibble on juicy kiwifruit from roadside orchards. Wander shorelines near perky volcanoes emerging from the Pacific Ocean — adventures for everyone!

HIGHLIGHTS

LISTEN FOR KIWI ROAMING WILD NEAR ŌHOPE BEACH

Explore one of the country's last remaining pōhutukawa forests at Ōhope Scenic Reserve during a nocturnal adventure, listening for kiwi and hunting for glowworms (p117).

DISAPPEAR BENEATH A CRAGGY HEADLAND INTO SUNBEAM-LIT CAVERNS

Descend steep staircases wedged between massive boulders to a sandy, pōhutukawa-shaded, secluded cove at Bowentown Heads near Waihi Beach, with cool caves to explore (p93).

A STEAMY WONDERLAND SURROUNDED BY APOCALYPTIC LANDSCAPES

Tick off spluttering vents and mud pools before traversing an iridescent thermal lake with barren trees poking through at Kuirau Park in Rotorua (p122).

WAIHI BEACH

OROKAWA BAY

Looping around headlands fringed with pōhutukawa, this coastal pathway leads to a secluded bay with a long, white, sandy beach.

At the northernmost point of Waihi Beach, a short beach walk past a small rocky outcrop leads to the trailhead. Then a 30-minute steady uphill trek passes through coastal forest, noisy with the courtship tunes of freshly hatched cicadas in summer. The hilly trail has spectacular views of the rolling waves below from cliff-top vantage points, but keep an eye on young explorers rushing ahead.

From the exposed headland, a short 15-minute amble downhill past kawakawa and tree ferns leads to Orokawa Bay, with lofty, windswept pōhutukawa trees providing pockets of shade for picnicking and wiling away a few hours. Sling a hammock between gnarly pōhutukawa branches and enjoy views of wildlife refuge Tūhua/Mayor Island perched in the Pacific Ocean.

Return the same way. Due to steep drop-offs, Orokawa Bay is unsafe for swimming. Take care during high tides and rough swells, as the trailhead can become inaccessible from the beach.

TŪHUA MAYOR ISLAND

Tūhua is the tip of an ancient, dormant volcano rising from the sea floor, which has erupted many times over the past 120,000 years — the last time about 6000 years ago. Its tumultuous volcanic past has created a unique set of landforms, including Opuahau, the highest peak at 355 metres above sea level. The volcanic crater contains two lakes near sea level: the green Lake Aroarotamahine and the almost black Lake Te Paritu.

image © Jane Johnsson

INFORMATION

GRADE: Easy/Medium.

ACCESSIBILITY: Well-graded track. During high tide or rough swells, the trailhead can become inaccessible.

TIME: Allow 45 min to 1 hour each way.

FACILITIES: Toilets at either end.

LOCATION: Parking on The Esplanade, Waihi Beach.

DOGS: No dogs.

BOWENTOWN HEADS

CAVE BAY

Out of sight beneath a craggy headland lies a secluded cove with tall, volcanic rock columns and small, sunbeam-lit caverns.

From the car park, descend steep staircases wedged between massive boulders to the sandy, pōhutukawa-shaded beach. The cave entrances are near the southern end, where enormous sun-bleached tree roots stretch between cliffs and into the lapping water — ideal for clambering over.

For the best experience, visit around low tide when most caves become accessible. Navigate volcanic rock pillars and walk among small caverns eroded by battering seas, now lit by sunbeams streaming through peepholes far above. The caves have great acoustics too.

Nearby, boats skilfully navigate the churning waters between Matakana Island and the headland. The island is a 20-kilometre-long sandspit covered in farms, orchards and forestry, and is home to only a couple of hundred residents year-round. Unfortunately, Cave Bay is not a swimming destination; the nearby, calm, harbour Anzac Bay is a better alternative.

INFORMATION

GRADE: Easy/Medium.

ACCESSIBILITY: Steep stairs, dirt path, rock-hopping and sandy beach.

TIME: 5 min one way.

FACILITIES: Toilets at Anzac Bay.

LOCATION: Bowentown Domain upper car park off Seaforth Road. The stairs start at the eastern side of the car park.

DOGS: On leads.

ATHENREE

ATHENREE WETLAND

When the appeal of beach-lazing wanes, a 20-minute stroll within Athenree Wildlife Refuge Reserve provides a leisurely alternative.

Binocular-toting bird-twitchers might glimpse threatened wetland species matuku/Australasian bittern, moho pererū/banded rail or tūturiwhatu/New Zealand dotterel.

Follow the wooden trail-makers past fresh- and saltwater ponds surrounded by regenerating shrubs and sprawling flax fields. The land was gifted by a local farmer, the late Maurice 'Snow' Garde-Browne.

INFORMATION: Allow 20 min to complete the 1 km loop. Flat grassy trail. No toilets. No dogs.

LOCATION: Parking is available off Steele Road between Athenree and Waihi Beach. Take it easy on the pot-holed road.

WAIHI BEACH

TRIG WALK & WATER RESERVOIR LOOP

For an accessible 20-minute adventure, the pretty Water Reservoir Loop provides a quick dose of nature where you can bring the pooch, buggy or zoom around on two wheels.

But for energetic folks keen to climb a hillside for commanding views of offshore volcanoes poking up in the bay, grab some sneakers and tick off Waihi Trig.

The well-trodden trail branches off the loop and steadily ascends broad, glute-burning steps beneath shady pines to multiple vantage points. Snap a selfie on the log photo frame, then continue to the trig for wrap-around coastal views.

INFORMATION: Allow 90 min (3 km) return. Well-graded trails and steps. Walking only to the trig; Reservoir Loop suitable for bikes and buggies. Toilets. Dogs on leads.

LOCATION: Signposted off Pacific Road.

BOWENTOWN HEADS

BOWENTOWN HEADS PĀ SITE

Many tribes have battled for this headland with its formidable views across the northern entrance of Tauranga Harbour. Terraces and large defensive ditches from two pā sites can still be seen, including Te Kura a Maia, which translates to 'training ground for young warriors'.

The steep trig path at the eastern end of the car park is suitable for walking or buggy-pushing extremists. After the first gut-busting paved section, grab a breather where it flattens off and watch boats navigate the often-rough channel between Matakana Island and the headland. Then allow another 5 minutes to the summit for postcard views of Bowentown Beach.

INFORMATION: Allow 15 min return. Toilets at Anzac Bay. Dogs on leads.

LOCATION: Parking is available at the Bowentown Domain upper car park, off Seaforth Road.

WAIHI

MARTHA MINE AND PIT RIM WALKWAY

On the southern edge of a vast mining chasm, a grand Gothic-styled Cornish Pumphouse overlooks a massive open pit, where over 1 million kilograms of precious metals have been unearthed.

INFORMATION

GRADE: Easy.

ACCESSIBILITY: Well-graded paths.

TIME: Allow 30 min for the southwestern highlights and 1 hour (about 4 km) for the loop.

FACILITIES: In Waihi township.

LOCATION: Parking on Seddon Street.

DOGS: Dogs on leads.

For those with limited time or energy, loitering near the 1904 pumphouse before a short jaunt west to the enormous Caterpillar 777 dump truck and views over the former open-cast mine should satisfy everyone.

A longer buggy- and bike-friendly adventure loops around the entire pit and passes historic mining relics and stands of kauri. Intriguingly, the loop also passes former residential areas evacuated due to subsidence after a house collapsed into a 50-metre by 15-metre hole in 2001.

In its heyday, Martha Mine was one of the world's most important underground gold and silver mines, before closing in 1952 due to falling gold prices, a lack of workers and outdated machinery. About 175,000 kilograms of gold and 1.2 million kilograms of silver had been extracted, from 12 million tonnes of ore. When gold prices increased in the 1980s, the mine resumed operations as a lower-cost open pit. However, open-cast mining operations have been on hold due to rockfall — the large slip visible on the North Wall happened in 2016.

In 2006, the three-storey, 1840-tonne historic pumphouse was shunted about 300 metres to its current location, on Teflon-coated concrete beams, after a collapsed historic shaft threatened the building.

SH2 KATIKATI
KAURI POINT JETTY

A 10-minute detour off SH2 leads to a long wooden jetty perched above turquoise waters, lapping the shoreline of pōhutukawa-smothered headlands.

Emerging from the shoreline beneath wizened trees, a 200-metre-long jetty provides a popular sun-soaked perch for seasoned and budding anglers to dangle a line. Trek along the narrow jetty and admire small headlands shaped by Māori tribes, and small, pōhutukawa-shaded coves.

Nearby, a pint-sized sheltered bay for sandcastle building, paddling and climbing over tangled tree roots is accessible from the lower car park along a 100-metre-long unmarked trail.

For a longer adventure, continue along the winding coastal path within Kauri Point Historical Reserve to Ōngare Point Road (about 45 minutes one way), taking in several pā sites. But for a short visit, the most fun, kid-friendly highlights are near the jetty.

INFORMATION

GRADE: Easy.

ACCESSIBILITY: Dirt path and wooden jetty.

TIME: Allow 30 min to 1 hour to explore.

FACILITIES: Toilet near the car park.

LOCATION: Parking at the end of Chelmsford Street.

DOGS: Dogs on leads.

PŌHUTUKAWA TREES

Pōhutukawa (*Metrosideros excelsa*) are fondly known as the New Zealand Christmas tree, which is about the time of year when they erupt into an impressive crimson display.

However, the tree is a tasty treat for possums, which eat many of them to death.

Young pōhutukawa grow at about 30 cm per year in height and 5–10 mm in diameter (thickness), while older trees grow about 10 cm a year and only 2 mm in diameter.

image © stock.adobe.com

FIND OUT MORE
projectcrimson.org.nz

SH2 KATIKATI

TUAHU KAURI LOOP

The drawcard for this stroll through a fern-lined valley is a double act of kauri trees which have stood their ground for more than six centuries.

INFORMATION

GRADE: Easy.

ACCESSIBILITY: Well-graded paths.

TIME: Allow 45 min (2.8 km) return.

FACILITIES: Toilet at the car park.

LOCATION: Parking at the end of Hot Springs Road, off SH2.

DOGS: No dogs.

Wander along well-groomed trails, which are easy-going underfoot, past bulbous nīkau palms and twittering birdlife. Stands of kauri 'rickers' aged between 30 and 50 years line the pathway, which gradually climbs into the foothills of Kaimai Mamaku Conservation Park.

Ignoring the first turnoff to the kauri trees, go left just 1 minute further along the trail to experience a more impressive arrival at the mighty natives. A wraparound platform allows you to get close to the kauri, some of the largest in the Bay of Plenty, and helps protect the 600-year-old trees' delicate feeding roots from being trampled and infected with kauri dieback.

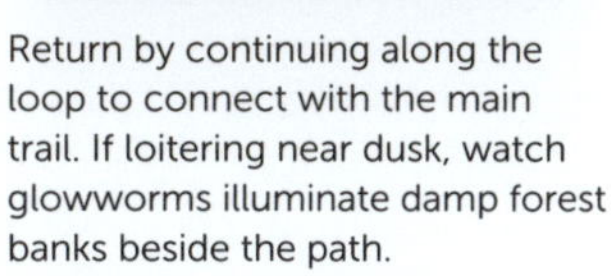

Return by continuing along the loop to connect with the main trail. If loitering near dusk, watch glowworms illuminate damp forest banks beside the path.

SENTINEL ROCK

For a couple of thigh-burning hours, extend the adventure by tramping to Sentinel Rock Lookout for spectacular views of Kaimai Mamaku Conservation Park. Allow 4–5 hours return. For the latest track updates, visit doc.govt.nz.

SH2 AONGATETE

AONGATETE WATERFALL

Flowing over shallow rock pools, this forest-shaded waterfall is ideal for summer bathing and bracing winter toe-dipping.

INFORMATION

GRADE: Easy/Medium.

ACCESSIBILITY: Generally well-graded dirt paths with steps and rocks. Both walks begin beside the gate, not across the field.

TIME: Allow 30–45 min one way to the swimming hole (about 1.7 km one way). Allow 20 min return for the nature walk from the car park.

FACILITIES: Toilets near the car park.

LOCATION: End of Wright Road, south of Katikati off SH2.

DOGS: No dogs.

Bring the togs for a dip in these secluded rock pools. Although warm days bring the crowds, there is plenty of space for everyone along the multi-tiered waterfall. The dense canopy of Kaimai Mamaku Conservation Park provides a picturesque backdrop for a half-day of picnicking, paddling and feeding the resident tuna/eels downstream.

The dirt trail is relatively rooty underfoot to begin but evens out beneath pūriri and kohekohe forest before descending through kauri groves to Aongatete Stream. Multiple trails wind through the forested valley, so double-check trail signs to avoid accidentally traversing the Kaimai Range.

NATURE TRAIL

Parallel to the main path, a short nature trail is worth exploring on the homeward stretch to keep kids engaged with critter and plant information and a wētā hotel.

KŌURA | CRAYFISH

Camouflaged with mottled dark-green shell-like skin, freshwater crayfish shelter among stones or burrow into muddy streambeds. During the day, only the occasional black beady eye or waving feeler can be spotted, as it's mostly at night when these scavengers emerge to feed on old leaves and small insects floating by. They don't hunt; they like food to be delivered!

Two species live in New Zealand: the North Island species (about 70 mm long), and the east and south of the South Island species (about 80 mm long).

FIND OUT MORE
quarrypark.org.nz

TAURANGA

TE PUNA QUARRY PARK

Transformed from an eyesore to a thriving hamlet of native and exotic plants, here kids can explore a tangled network of pathways while searching for an enormous dragon.

INFORMATION

GRADE: Easy.

ACCESSIBILITY: Dirt paths, boardwalks and steps. Buggy-friendly on the main path. Open daily and free to enter, but donations are appreciated.

TIME: Allow 1 hour for a quick visit. Twice as long for free-range exploring.

FACILITIES: Toilets available.

LOCATION: At the end of Quarry Road off SH2, 15 km west of Tauranga.

DOGS: Dogs on leads.

The former quarry was such a prominent landmark on the Minden Hills that even boaties used it as a wayfinding point. But after two decades of hard graft by green-thumbed volunteers, the vast rock amphitheatre has undergone a dramatic revival.

To get a lay of the land of the 32-hectare park's nooks and crannies, grab an information map on arrival and take the 45-minute garden loop. Alternatively, free-range on unmarked trails past arid cactus banks, fragrant herbs, the butterfly garden or South African botanicals. For art buffs, there're nearly 50 outdoor sculptures to appreciate. Wooden shelters provide refuge from blistering hot days or rainstorms.

At the turn of the century, hundreds of wild goats grazed the scrappy landscape covered in gorse, woolly nightshade and pines. But when the pines were logged and the goats removed, king ferns returned, and after more than 5000 native trees and shrubs were planted, the bush is self-seeding and regenerating.

KIHIKIHI-WAWĀ CHORUS CICADA

After living underground for up to five years, newly emerged chorus cicadas shed their shells before beginning their courtship rituals. In February, when their population peaks, it can be deafening, as the males compete with the loudest and most musical songs. Females lay eggs on tree branches which can take up to 10 months to hatch before the larvae burrow into the ground to become nymphs. After reaching their maximum size, they climb back up the tree and discard their shells. The chorus cicada is the most common species of cicada in New Zealand.

SH2 WHAKAMĀRAMA

PUKETOKI RESERVE

Remnants of historic logging endeavours lie scattered alongside the trail, with a replica bogie waiting to clamber over — an easily explored, kid-friendly bush adventure.

INFORMATION

GRADE: Easy.

ACCESSIBILITY: Well-graded paths. Steps on the long adventure.

TIME: Allow 20 min for the short loop or 1 hour for the long loop.

FACILITIES: Toilet.

LOCATION: Turn off SH2 onto Barrett Road, then take Whakamārama Road to Leyland Road. There is plenty of parking beside the reserve entrance.

DOGS: Dogs on leads.

During the early 1900s, a bustling logging enterprise operated within this now peaceful forest remnant. Tramways carted felled native trees to the coast near Whakamārama, where waiting barges transported the prized timber to Auckland. In 1926, Henry Sharplin of the Whakamarama Land & Timber Company donated 34 hectares of forest to the local community. After a few decades of hard graft by volunteers, the formerly sparse landscape is home to native birds and other critters, with fungi growing beside the trail. Tame toutouwai/North Island robins often flit close to humans hiking.

For a quick bush experience, the well-graded shorter loop suits young explorers. Alternatively,

the longer, more undulating trail explores deeper into the forest past frond-laden tree ferns and sizeable natives that escaped logging. Neither option is strenuous, and both pass hundreds of thriving epiphytes clinging tightly to the forest canopy high above.

Cool off in the shallow Te Puna Stream beside the car park after adventuring.

FOREST FLOOR DWELLERS

DISCOVER FUNGI IN NATIVE FORESTS

Fungi are pretty amazing things. They live on dark, damp forest floors and don't need sunlight to grow because they don't use light energy to fuel themselves. There are about 7300 identified species of fungi in New Zealand.

MOUNT MAUNGANUI

TE ARA TŪTANGA/MAUAO BASE TRACK

This coastal pathway looping around the sacred Mauao/Mount Maunganui offers plenty of ocean views, easy strolling and the occasional marine wildlife encounter.

Circling the mighty extinct volcano is an accessible trail wedged between the steep mountainside and rocky shoreline. Sheltered by arching pōhutukawa erupting in crimson flowers from about mid-November, the wide, flat pathway passes from sheltered Pilot Bay to the edge of the Pacific Ocean. Keep an eye out for well-camouflaged seals lounging on the rocks or bobbing on waves.

If the summit of Mauao isn't on the list, this adventure runs an excellent close second, providing landscape and ocean views as you soak up the coastal vibe of this landmark. Try to time a visit with the arrival of a colossal cruise ship as it passes incredibly close to Mauao while deftly navigating through the narrow harbour channel. Bonus: finish the adventure by refuelling the troops with ice creams on the beach.

Mauao means 'caught by the dawn', and visiting at either end of the day for sunrise or sunset makes the adventure more memorable.

MAUAO SUMMIT WALK

If the 232-metre-high summit of Mauao beckons, prepare for a sweaty climb up its flanks. It's not an easy climb, and little kids will struggle if self-powered — popping them into a backpack will help. Walk past the surf-lifesaving club and choose between two options: the more direct yet steeper Waikorire Track climbs staircases, while the Oruahine Track winds around the northern side, with views of Matakana Island. Allow 30 to 40 min one way for both options. No dogs.

INFORMATION:

GRADE: Easy.

ACCESSIBILITY: Well-graded paths.

TIME: Allow 45 min (3.4 km) for the loop.

FACILITIES: Toilets beside the surf club and Pilot Bay boat ramp.

LOCATION: On-street parking is available near Pilot Bay Beach.

DOGS: No dogs.

MOUNT MAUNGANUI

MOTURIKI | LEISURE ISLAND

This extinct volcano is the more accessible cousin of Mauao and provides a quick, salt-laden breezy adventure.

From the main Mount Maunganui beach, cross the artificial land-bridge to this small island covered in twisty-trunked pōhutukawa. Only a few glimpses of the island's colourful history — as a quarry, Māori pā, fun park with hydroslides and even a marine aquarium with dolphins — are visible. Today, numerous little trails snake up and over the nearly 2.5-hectare island leading to its northernmost tip, where the imposing bluffs of Mauao/ Mount Maunganui are on show, and a blowhole delivers a thrilling display during high tides.

The island is often heaving with visitors in mid-summer due to its easy access and wide, shallow steps with only a few rooty sections. The island juts out past the breakers crashing onto the main beach, so keen grommets can be seen wholeheartedly attacking the surf.

INFORMATION:

GRADE: Easy.

ACCESSIBILITY: Dirt paths, steps and rocky outcrop.

TIME: Allow 30 min return.

FACILITIES: Toilets nearby.

LOCATION: On-street parking on Marine Parade, Mount Maunganui.

DOGS: No dogs.

BROOKFIELD

WAIKAREAO ESTUARY WALKWAY

Explore wide boardwalks surrounded by a tidal wetland and expansive harbour views on foot or two wheels. From the wooden lookout perched among the mangroves, watch for kōtare/sacred kingfisher, poaka/pied stilts and tōrea pango/variable oystercatchers stalking through the soggy landscape, and at low tide watch little crabs scurrying around searching for dinner. The walkway begins from multiple points, although the scenic Maxwells Road entrance offers kawakawa- and rimu-lined paths with estuary views fringed with raupō and cabbage trees. It also has grassy banks for picnics and there's a nearby estuary for wading. If you don't fancy the entire loop, which includes a lengthy section beside the noisy Takitimu Drive (SH2), turn around at any point for a shorter out-and-back adventure.

INFORMATION: Allow 2 hours (8.2 km) to walk the whole loop; 1 hour to bike. Toilets are available along the way. Dogs on leads.

LOCATION: Parking is available off Maxwells Road near Chapel Street, Otūmoetai.

image © Tourism Bay of Plenty

PARKVALE

TUTARAWĀNANGA/ YATTON PARK

A buggy-friendly path loops around this small headland jutting into Waimapu Estuary, with plenty of other short detours through bamboo forests for older explorers.

Stroll to the easternmost tip for views of the estuary and steps descending to the shoreline, where wading birds hide in the shallows. Or continue along the main path through native and exotic trees with labels for the botanically minded. Allow time to explore the traditional garden area beside Fraser Street with its bubbling waterfall, flower gardens and nearby playground.

A smattering of picnic tables and bench seats throughout the park are popular hangouts for family gatherings.

INFORMATION: Allow 30 min return. Toilets. Dogs on leads.

LOCATION: Car park entry off Fraser Street, Parkvale. Check gate closure times on arrival.

BETHLEHEM

GORDON CARMICHAEL RESERVE

Easy, flat trails weave through this 60-hectare stormwater reserve, providing a nature adventure with minimal effort. Buggies and kids on two wheels can easily navigate the well-graded wetland trails, which loop together into various distances suiting all ages and energy levels.

For some quick highlights, head north from the western edge of the car park and turn right to loop around in an anti-clockwise direction back to the car park.

The reserve has multiple entry points, but the Carmichael Road entrance, with its playground and barbecue area, is popular with visitors during long summer evenings. Extend your adventure by visiting nearby York Park.

INFORMATION: Allow 30 min return walking. Toilets. Dogs on leads.

LOCATION: Carmichael Road, Bethlehem.

BY THE SEA

SHORELINE AND ROCK POOLS

Battered by the tides and blistering-hot summers, the creatures that call the shoreline and shallow rock pools home are some of the hardiest in New Zealand. Not only do they face the surging ocean every day, but they also risk becoming a tasty morsel for passing birds when the tide retreats and their watery home becomes shallower and less able to protect them. Rock pools are great spots to observe crabs, fish and snails, although you may need to patiently wait while they emerge from hiding under rocks and in crevices.

1. KĀUNGA | HERMIT CRABS

These hungry little scavengers make their homes in abandoned snail shells. They feed at night on algae and detritus (debris and dead matter) that floats down through the ocean. During the day they are often spotted in rock pools. When they grow, they 'moult' their shell to find a bigger shell to protect them. This often involves trading shells with other crabs, after they've both probed and rocked their potential homes to check for suitability. Hermit crabs are vulnerable to predators because of their thin shells.

image © Kat Bolstad

2. NEPTUNE'S NECKLACE

This bubbly-looking seaweed is commonly found in rock pools at mid-tide levels throughout New Zealand and Australia. It's often brown, although can be orange or green in colour, too. It feels slimy to touch, and the slime helps it stay moist when exposed to air. The beads are filled with gas which allows them to rise to the surface and obtain sunlight, and water which keeps them hydrated. Also known as sea grapes or bubbleweed.

3. TIOTIO | BARNACLES

These intriguing critters start life as a shrimp-like creature that finds a spot to call home by cementing its head onto a rock. Over time, it builds a limestone structure that has a trapdoor on top that the barnacle can open and shut. It waves its hairy legs in the water to catch unsuspecting plankton floating by. If it's successful, it drags the plankton back into its shell before devouring it.

4. KAPU PARAHUA CUSHION STARFISH

These starfish are the most likely to be spotted along the coastline and in tidal rock pools. They can live for 10 years, and scavenge on living and dead organisms by extending their stomach outside of their body to cover and digest their prey. They usually have five arms and look as spongy as a soft cushion. They come in plenty of different colours: red, orange and pink through to bluish-green and black.

LET LOOSE ON

TAURANGA PLAYGROUNDS

TAURANGA SOUTH

MEMORIAL PARK

So much to do! Chug around the park on the miniature railway (Sundays from 10am to 3pm) or let kids loose on this seaside park with swing bridges, ropes course and tunnels. Don't miss zipping down the rocket-ship slide, the mini-putt course or splashing about in the giant fountain.

LOCATION: Parking at the end of Fraser Street or off Seventh Avenue, Tauranga South.

CITY CENTRE

THE STRAND RESERVE

Splish-splash summer away while darting between shooting water jets, before tackling the marine-themed playground packed full of characters from Hairy Maclary storybooks, a pier with a bombing platform, rope swings and a pirate fortress. And for the brave, two steep slides!

LOCATION: Car park off Dive Crescent.

PYES PA

PAKANGA RESERVE/ THE LAKES WATERPARK

Kids can chase water flowing along narrow wooden and concrete channels to a giant Archimedes' screw — watch water defy gravity! A fantastic park with loads of opportunities to get soaked and have fun — bring a change of clothes. Shaded seating areas and a small playground are nearby.

LOCATION: Pakanga Grove, Pyes Pa.

OTŪMOETAI

KULIM PARK

This picturesque waterfront playground has swings, climbing forts and a half basketball court. Clamber up the small hill to jump on the slide. Waving train buffs might get a toot from drivers chugging past. Bring togs to paddle in the sheltered bay.

LOCATION: Kulim Avenue, Otūmoetai

PYES PA

CASLANI RESERVE

A crowd-pleasing 40-metre-long flying fox draws crowds looking for a thrilling ride. Younger kids will enjoy rope swings, a seesaw and slides before tearing along little tunnels beneath grassy mounds — this pretty lakeside playground has something for all ages.

LOCATION: Opposite The Lakes Shopping Village on Caslani Lane, Pyes Pa.

WELCOME BAY

JOHNSON RESERVE

This sheltered reserve, with its humpy boardwalk bridges and paths winding past swampy streams with kahikatea trees and raupō/bulrush, is accessible from multiple entry points. But the bonus of starting at Waipuna Park is the playground, and a walnut grove for kids to try their hand at nut collecting.

Explorers can tear around the short loops or walk its entire length — taking a photo of the park map near the entrance helps navigation. Peer off the boardwalks to spot aquatic critters darting through the streams.

INFORMATION: Allow 30 min to 1 hour to explore. Walking only. Toilets. Dogs on leads. Half basketball court. Playground and walnut grove.

LOCATION: Waipuna Park, Kaitemako Road, Welcome Bay.

TAURANGA

KOPURERERUA VALLEY WALKWAY

Discover one of Australasia's largest urban wetlands, an impressive 300 hectares of sprawling wetlands, native bushland, farmland, ponds and waterways. Various trails wind through the valley — boardwalks to gravel pathways — passing archaeological sites, including mounded pā sites.

Explore on two wheels or tackle bite-sized walking adventures while watching swooping kāhu/swamp harriers hunting prey among the flax and streamside shrubbery. Paths west of the expressway are more shaded, or opt for the eastern routes with sweeping wetland views.

INFORMATION: Visit Tauranga.govt.nz for a trail map. Dogs on leads.

LOCATION: There are multiple starting points and facilities within the valley.

image © Tourism Bay of Plenty.

MATUA

MATUA SALTMARSH WETLANDS

Choose to explore deep within this 21-hectare coastal wetland on boardwalks snaking between mangroves, or tick off kid-friendly highlights near its western shoreline. From Bay Street, head east on the wetland's newest boardwalk, hopefully spotting a moho pererū/banded rail or mātātā/fernbird stalking through the shallows. Explorers can dangle legs off the small wooden jetty jutting out into the estuary. From here, continue for a longer adventure or exit onto Sunny Bay Road (a relatively steep concrete path) to loop back along quiet streets to the car.

INFORMATION: Allow 30 min for the short loop. The longer option is an out-and-back, so turn around when little legs tire. Dogs on leads. Suitable for bikes, buggies and wheelchairs.

LOCATION: Bay Street.

TE RAE O PAPAMOA

PAPAMOA HILLS REGIONAL PARK

Climb the flanks of this maunga along sweeping, sun-drenched pathways, past archaeological sites dating back nearly 400 years.

INFORMATION

GRADE: Medium.

ACCESSIBILITY: Dirt paths, steps and farmland.

TIME: Allow 1 hour return or 90 min with younger kids.

FACILITIES: Toilets at the car park.

LOCATION: From Pacific Coast Highway/Te Puke Highway, turn onto Poplar Lane. About 20 km from Tauranga. The car park is locked overnight.

DOGS: No dogs.

The pulse-quickening first 500 metres of this adventure climb steeply from the car park along a dirt path before levelling out after the stile. Then broad switchbacks give tantalising glimpses of the summit and views across berry orchards surrounded by farmland stretching to the Bay of Plenty coast. Grab a breather on benches beside the trail if needed.

The 135-hectare park has a steady stream of visitors — some come for the views, others for the grunty workout, or to explore six pā sites. The park's cultural heritage dates back more than 350 years, and over 2000 archaeological features have been unearthed among the rolling hills. If choosing to adventure 'off-piste' on the operational farm to view the pā sites, remember to leave gates as found.

The park's most popular walk ends on the flat summit of Karangaumu, 224 metres above sea level, with wraparound views of the busy regional port, horticultural landscape and long, sandy shoreline. Visit early morning for sun-mottled ocean views or at dusk for Mauao/Mount Maunganui bathed in sunset colours. Return the same way.

IMPORTANT

The car park gates are closed overnight. Check closure times on arrival. The steep path is unsuitable for jandals and can be slippery going downhill. Remember sunscreen, water and hats, as this exposed mountain is a summer heat-trap.

ŌROPI

ŌTANEWAINUKU FOREST/RIMU LOOP WALK

Experience an ancient forest filled with towering rimu trees rising through the canopy, untouched by the ravages of logging. Starting from opposite the small shelter, the generally well-graded trail dips straight into a virgin forest with mighty rimu growing within arm's reach of the pathway. More than 300 plant species grow here, including the rare tree daisy kohurangi/Kirk's daisy perched high within the old-growth forest canopy. It's also home to North Island brown kiwi, kōkako and pekapeka-tou-roa/long-tailed bats, thanks to pest eradication efforts by Ōtanewainuku Kiwi Trust volunteers. The loop finishes beside the road, about 100 metres from the car park.

INFORMATION: Allow about 45 min to 1 hour (about 1.7 km) for the loop. Small shelter, toilet and picnic area. No dogs.

LOCATION: 20 km south of Tauranga on Mountain Road, Ōropi.

TE PUKE

RAPARAPAHOE STREAM

Squeezing its way through a narrow, bush-clad gorge, the Raparapahoe Stream cascades over a 3-metre-high bank into a sprawling watering hole — ideal for summer dipping.

The challenging trail is rooty and rough in a few sections and includes multiple stairs while zigzagging steeply into the bush-covered gorge. Then the path flattens while continuing upstream past mossy boulders for about 5 to 10 minutes to the base of the sheer cliff face.

Bring the togs and snacks, and enjoy a few hours paddling in the refreshing water and watching brave kids plunge off the rocks.

INFORMATION: Walking only. Allow 1 hour (about 2 km) return. No facilities. Dogs on leads.

LOCATION: About 30 minutes from Tauranga. No. 4 Road, Te Puke.

PAPAMOA

KAITUNA WETLAND

Clumps of raupō/bulrush and tī kouka/cabbage trees line the raised 4WD track within this wetland, which can be explored quickly, at a more leisurely pace or even on kayaks. Opting for the 2-kilometre short loop (40 min return) takes in the bird hide, or stretch the legs on the 4.4-kilometre loop (about 75 min return) to explore deeper into the biggest original wetland remaining in the Bay of Plenty.

Cross the stile from the car park for the short and long loops or explore the wetlands from water level on kayaks — multiple portage spots allow paddlers deep into the wetlands. Keep an eye on the left after about 10 minutes for the camouflaged hide — bring binoculars to feel among the avian action. Threatened mātātā/fernbird, pūweto/spotless crake and matuku/Australasian bittern live here.

INFORMATION: No dogs. Avoid during duck-hunting season.

LOCATION: At the junction of Kaituna and Pah Roads, Papamoa.

PAPAMOA

KAIATE FALLS | TE REREKAWAU FALLS

Visit a pair of waterfalls plunging down a ravine surrounded by steep, bush-clad slopes, with views of Mauao/Mount Maunganui on the horizon.

INFORMATION:

GRADE: Easy/Medium.

ACCESSIBILITY: Dirt paths, steps and slippery rocks after rain.

TIME: Allow 45 min to 1 hour return.

FACILITIES: Toilet at the car park.

LOCATION: About a 30-minute drive from Tauranga. Kaiate Falls Road, Waitao.

DOGS: On leads.

Along the 10-minute walk from the car park, you will hear the cascading tiers of the upper waterfall before they come into view, surrounded by native forest. And although they are picturesque, the lower, 15-metre-high waterfall is where the crowds form. Follow the dirt trail downstream, shaded year-round by a dense canopy, with Kaiate Stream never out of earshot.

The main event plunges off a steep ignimbrite bluff into a pool surrounded by rock faces and ferns — a neat picnic destination. Clamber up carved stone steps and feel chilly winds and spray blasting from the falls, providing a cool dousing in summer. After rain, this adventure becomes a lush oasis, with waterlogged moss and drooping ferns weighed down by water droplets.

Although the steady descent to the lower falls means a solid climb back to the car park, it is very doable with little ones — just allow extra time. Exit the lower valley over the small footbridge — look for the chasms created by eroding water — and climb along pathways and steps lined by well-munched kawakawa (p54). Seats provide respite and an opportunity to watch pīwakawaka/fantails flitting nearby. Views of the picturesque volcanic cone of Mauao (p102) appear through gaps in the forest.

IMPORTANT

Please read the water quality and safety signs beside the car park.

SH36 BETWEEN TAURANGA AND ROTORUA

TECT PARK

Vast adventure zones cater for almost all outdoorsy activities, from horse riding to rally-car driving to sedate bike rides, within this 1650-hectare park halfway between Tauranga and Rotorua.

INFORMATION

GRADE: Easy.

ACCESSIBILITY: Well-graded trails.

TIME: Uno 15 to 20 min, Kererū 20 to 30 min.

FACILITIES: Toilets and shelter.

LOCATION: Halfway between Tauranga and Rotorua on SH36. Open during daylight hours.

DOGS: Dogs on leads. Off-lead area available.

There are some fantastic two-wheel adventures for kids throughout the park, regardless of how experienced they are in the saddle. Follow the signs off SH36 to the mountain biking hub and warm up the legs on the short dirt loop beside the car park shelter before disappearing into the forest on two nearby kid-friendly trails. For beginner mountain bike riders, the Uno trail (above image) is an excellent introduction, beneath the tree canopy on soft, pine-needle-cushioned trails and gently sloping dirt berms. Looking for more? The slightly longer Kererū track loops along the park's northern fringes before winding back into the car park.

Relax and refuel at the Lost Tank picnic area overlooking the valley — about a 10-minute walk or 5-minute bike from the car park. Grab a park map from the shelter to find the trailhead near the southern side of the car park. The 1-kilometre return trail pops out beside a water tank and picnic table with scenic views. Check gate closure times on arrival.

TE RERENGA TRAIL

Meander through various landscapes on this walking-only loop beneath native forest, past felled forestry to a 60-metre-long, hand-dug tunnel beneath SH36 before heading home again. The pathway dips beneath giant pine trees from the car park leading to the tunnel — stay quiet to see the glowworms and cave wētā living on the tunnel roof. The trail has stairs, some steeper sections and follows alongside Te Rerenga Stream on boardwalks. Allow 1 hour to 90 minutes to explore the 2.5-kilometre adventure.

FIND OUT MORE
tectpark.co.nz

WHAKATĀNE

WHITE PINE BUSH

Amble beneath stands of huge kahikatea trees, some centuries old, and imagine how the wetlands of the Rangitāiki Plains once looked smothered in dense native forests.

INFORMATION

GRADE: Easy.

ACCESSIBILITY: The well-graded trail is suitable for buggies and assisted wheelchair users.

TIME: Allow 15 minutes (about 250 m) for the loop.

FACILITIES: Picnic table by the entrance.

LOCATION: White Pine Bush Road (SH2), between Awakeri and Tāneatua, 20 km south of Whakatāne.

DOGS: No dogs.

Kahikatea (once known as white pine) are the giants of New Zealand forests, and historically their pale, odourless timber was considered ideal for boxes for exporting butter, as it did not taint the produce during long journeys overseas. Luckily, the majestic trees poking through the canopy of the 4.5-hectare White Pine Bush Scenic Reserve were spared from becoming butter boxes during forest clearance in the late 1880s. Take a glimpse into New Zealand history with these 300-year-old beauties soaring 40 metres high with huge trunks.

The easy, flat pathway loops around large, buttressed kahikatea roots sheltered by drooping nīkau fronds, tawa and pukatea. Korimako/bellbird, riroriro/grey warbler and tahou/silvereye are often spied flittering among the climbing rātā and supplejack.

GUMBOOT FENCE

Bring along a gumboot to donate to the iconic gumboot fence near the entrance, with gumboots of all sizes decorated with cheerful, funny quotes.

WHAKATĀNE SKATEPARK

Skate through a world of Māori mythology while carving the gaping mouth of a colourful taniwha, as dreamed up by local artist Te Marunui Hotene. Conquer plenty of street elements and smooth flows to the open-end bowl, surrounded by motifs reflecting nearby traditional flax-dyeing pools and the estuary — all close to the Whakatāne River on McAlister Street. For another option, head to Ōpōtiki for skateboarding thrills on the fantastic pump track and skatepark on Potts Avenue.

WHAKATĀNE

MOKORUA BUSH BIRD WALK

Tall native trees shade the pathway that climbs — at times steeply — to a ridgeline in Mokorua Bush Scenic Reserve, home to North Island kiwi and plenty of other native birds. The trail connects Gorge Road near the junction with Valley Road with White Horse Drive, with a 15-minute-walk road section to complete the loop (or arrange transport at either end). There are fewer steps to climb from the White Horse Drive end, and it's also buggy-friendly until the bridge for a quick 20-minute return adventure. Look for healthy-sized tuna/eel lounging in the stream. This is a pretty nature walk through coastal forest.

INFORMATION: Allow 45 min to 1 hour for the walk. Allow 15 min for the 1.3-km road section. Well-graded trail with steps. No dogs.

LOCATION: Plenty of parking off Gorge Road or White Horse Drive, Whakatāne.

WHAKATĀNE

KIWI WANDERING TRAIL

Wander through the 'Kiwi Capital of the World' on a self-guided urban scavenger hunt searching for 10 life-size bronze statues. Find Big Al with his transmitter; Pea, the first kiwi chick to hatch and grow up naturally in the wild in the Whakatāne Kiwi Project; or discover how Two Toes lost his toes! Along the way, learn about the small but mighty kiwi who have been part of the project's breeding programme.

Wairaka Centennial Park has an excellent playground and splash-pad for kids to cool off on. Nearby is a sheltered area for paddling or poking around in the estuary if the tide is out. Download a trail map from whakatanekiwi.org.nz.

INFORMATION: Allow 1 hour return (about 1.6 km one way).

LOCATION: Starts at Te Kōputu a Te Whanga a Toi — Whakatāne Library and Exhibition Centre off Kakahoroa Drive and finishes at Wairaka Centennial Park.

WHAKATĀNE

TE ANA O MURIWAI/ MURIWAI'S CAVE

Flanked by wooden carvings and kawakawa bushes, this cave once extended 122 metres into the hillside and is one of the region's most sacred and historically significant sites. It was one of three landmarks Toroa, the captain of the *Mataatua* waka, was told to look for by his father Irākewa when searching for Whakatāne. (The other two were Te Wairere Falls (p115) and Te Toka o Irākewa/ Irākewa Rock at the entrance to the Whakatāne Harbour.) The cave became home to Muriwai, the sister of Toroa, who was renowned for her wisdom. Although partially collapsed now, the small, shallow cave once accommodated up to 60 people and remains a significant historical site.

INFORMATION: Open 24 hours. Allow 5 min.

LOCATION: Near 35 Muriwai Drive, Whakatāne.

images © @Whakatāne.nz.

ŌHOPE

ŌTARAWAIRERE BEACH

Hidden behind a headland from the popular Ōhope Beach and accessible only on foot or across glistening waters on kayaks, you can avoid the masses on this secluded beach.

INFORMATION

GRADE: Medium.

ACCESSIBILITY: Well-graded dirt trails with steep stairs.

TIME: From Ōhope Beach, allow 25 minutes. From Ōtarawairere Road, allow 15 minutes. Times are one-way.

FACILITIES: Toilet at the beach. BYO toilet paper, just in case.

LOCATION: Trails start from West End Road, Ōhope Beach, and beside 117 Ōtarawairere Road, Ōhope.

DOGS: No dogs.

Laze beneath sprawling pōhutukawa trees while the kids splash in clear waters lapping the crushed-seashell beach. At low tide, explore rock pools inhabited by colourful starfish and aquatic critters or bring snorkels to see what lurks beneath the sparkling water's surface. Although this sheltered beach feels remote, this slice of coastal bliss is within easy walking distance of Ōhope Beach.

There are two main options for accessing the beach. From the western end of Ōhope Beach, the walkway climbs to a peninsula with views across the bay, past Ōhope to Whangaparāoa/Cape Runaway in the distance, before descending through native bush to emerge on the shimmering shoreline. Or opt for the shorter option near the end of Ōtarawairere Road, which descends directly to the beach. Both options include steps and some steep sections.

The nearby signposted Kohi Point lookout is worth detouring to for views across the Whakatāne River and township.

NGĀ TAPUWAE O TOI TRAIL

Instead of adventuring in short bursts, tackle this 16-kilometre-long trail winding beneath native bush, past historic pā sites and along stunning clifftops with ocean views to the secluded Ōtarawairere Beach. Allow 5 to 7 hours for this adventure that passes through three scenic reserves: Kohi Point, Ōhope and Mokorua. No dogs. Walking only.

Before visiting, download a trail map and check for any trail closures at doc.govt.nz.

TE WAIRERE FALLS

This sacred waterfall plunges off the hillside almost within earshot of the main street. It is one of three landmarks that voyager Toroa was instructed to find by his father while searching for Whakatāne. This landmark has endured throughout history and supported local industry, with several flax and flour mills built nearby in the 1870s. It also supplied water to the township until the 1920s. Bathing and eating nearby is discouraged due to its cultural importance to the Ngāti Awa people. It's almost visible from the car park, but a less-than-one-minute stroll leads to its rocky base, with views of the impressive multi-tiered waterfall. Visit at night to see the lights.

INFORMATION: Allow 5 minutes.

LOCATION: Toroa Street.

PUKETAPU LOOKOUT

Get the lay of the land from the same lookout that Ngāti Awa iwi used for over 600 years. From the grassy vantage point, tick off highlights surrounding the coastal township: Moutohorā/Whale Island, New Zealand's only active marine volcano Whakaari/White Island, and watch Whakatāne River entering the Pacific Ocean past the iconic bronze statue of Wairaka, the 'Lady on the Rock'.

For a longer, more step-filled adventure, start from Canning Place up the world's first 'vertigraph', with 43 glazed tiles forming an image of flora and fauna. Then there's a quick roadside walk to the trailhead at the junction between Hillcrest Road and Seaview Road.

INFORMATION: Allow 15 min return or 30 min return from Canning Street. Both options have steep concrete paths with steps.

LOCATION: Seaview Road car park or Canning Place.

ŌHOPE HARBOURSIDE TRAIL

Pedal alongside a vast estuary with serene views of Ōhiwa Harbour, past wading birds escaping chillier arctic homelands. Flat, wide trails follow the harbour's edge, providing a leisurely outing on two wheels or a sedate stroll to explore the tidal landscape. The trail passes through a few harbourside reserves, including Otao Reserve, with a playground and toilet. There is nothing strenuous here, so enjoy a leisurely hour or so in the saddle. For a breather, stop beside the shoreline and poke around in the estuary, looking for mud-dwelling molluscs. Return the same way on the out-and-back dual-use pathway or follow quiet residential streets back to the start.

INFORMATION: Open 24 hours. Allow 1 hour (about 3 km one way) return. Dogs on leads.

LOCATION: Start either at Waterways Drive or Port Ōhope Wharf, Port Ōhope.

image © @Whakatāne.nz.

ŌHIWA HARBOUR

NUKUHOU SALTMARSH & RIVER WALK

A saltmarsh surrounding the Nukuhou River mouth as it enters the Ōhiwa Harbour can be explored by a boardwalk, past secretive birds hiding in the shallows.

INFORMATION

GRADE: Easy.

ACCESSIBILITY: Well-graded dirt trails and boardwalk. Outdoorsy buggies will cope on the lookout pathway.

TIME: Allow 15 min for the lookout or 1 hour return for the entire walkway.

FACILITIES: None.

LOCATION: Wainui Road, Ōhiwa Harbour. Halfway between Whakatāne and Ōpōtiki.

DOGS: No dogs.

Take a short, 5-minute walk from the car park to a lookout on the saltmarsh fringes for a glimpse of this 60-hectare ecosystem. The mingling of mangroves and saltmarsh vegetation near the river mouth is home to many birds; perhaps spy the at-risk mātātā/fernbird or other coastal birds fossicking for crabs and worms. Keen birders have spied more than 50 species in the area, from kōtare/sacred kingfisher to tara/white-fronted terns.

For a longer adventure, a 2-kilometre pathway partially hugging Wainui Road leads to an īnanga/whitebait-spawning area near the river mouth, with ceramic artworks of native birds along the way. Some parts of this pathway are a little rough underfoot, but a short, fun option on winding boardwalks between raupō/bulrush starts opposite Cheddar Valley Pottery — where the colourful tiles are made. Head east for an out-and-back 15-minute adventure.

MATUKU MOANA
REEF HERON

These stealthy native birds stalk around rocky shorelines and estuary mudflats on the hunt for small critters, including crustaceans, worms and small fish. Most of the nationally endangered bird's 300 to 500 population live in the northern areas of the North Island.

Reef herons look similar to the white-faced heron but are dark grey, and less commonly spotted. They are very wary and will fly away if approached too closely.

ŌHOPE

FAIRBROTHER LOOP WALK

Explore one of the country's largest remaining coastal pōhutukawa forests. Don't miss returning for a nocturnal adventure, listening for wild kiwi calls and hunting for glowworms.

INFORMATION

GRADE: Medium.

ACCESSIBILITY: Dirt paths with steps.

TIME: Allow 1 hour return.

FACILITIES: Toilets at Ōhope Beach.

LOCATION: The trail starts beneath the waharoa/carved archway near the junction of Pacific Coast Highway and West End Road, Ōhope.

DOGS: No dogs.

During the day, take in the highlights of this patch of Ōhope Scenic Reserve with its nīkau palms and old pōhutukawa. A loop climbs steadily to a ridgeline along well-graded dirt pathways with plenty of steps. Take either trail at the junction 5 minutes from the car park, although the clockwise route initially has fewer steps to climb. Watch for the ground-feeding toutouwai/North Island robin following you, take a breather at the grove of nīkau or watch the white breakers on the 11-kilometre-long Ōhope Beach.

At night, listen for the nocturnal calls of kiwi and ruru/morepork. More than 300 kiwi live close to Whakatāne and the best time to hear them is between April and July. Plenty of tuna/eels in the streams can be spied, slithering along in the dark water, or look for large sheetweb spiders hanging beneath webs up to half a metre across, and wētā with spiny legs poking out.

Download a trail map and guided night tour dates from whakatanekiwi.org.nz.

RURU | MOREPORK

Flying silently under cover of darkness, these nocturnal hunters are looking for wētā, moths and spiders to catch with their large sharp talons or beaks. They nest in tree cavities or high in trees among clumps of epiphytes during the day. In Māori tradition, they are seen as watchful guardians belonging to the spirit world. Listen out for their haunting call in forests throughout mainland New Zealand. The females are bigger than the males and measure about 30 cm head to tail. Their heads can turn through 270 degrees!

WAIOTAHE

ONEKAWA TE MAWHAI REGIONAL PARK

Climb to two historic pā sites on a headland with formidable views of the surrounding landscape, the Pacific Ocean and Ōhiwa Harbour.

INFORMATION

GRADE: Medium.

ACCESSIBILITY: Gravel and grassy paths.

TIME: Allow 45 min to 1 hour return to Onekawa pā from Bryans Road.

FACILITIES: No facilities on the eastern side. Toilet at Ōhiwa Reserve.

LOCATION: Parking at the end of Bryans Road off Ōhiwa Beach Road, or near the end of Ōhiwa Harbour Road on the park's western side.

DOGS: Dogs on leads.

There are a couple of ways to explore this nearly 27-hectare regional park alongside Ōhiwa Harbour. On its western flanks, spend a half day exploring the harbourside, longer trails and a collection of rare coastal plants.

Or head to Bryans Road car park on the park's eastern side for the quickest route to a vantage point with views of waves surging inland and the Pacific Ocean stretching to the horizon. From the car park, veer off the southern loop (which takes 90 minutes to 2 hours to complete) onto the steep grassy trail, partially shaded by pōhutukawa spilling down the hillside. After the short uphill section, the path becomes a grassy 4WD track wedged between paddocks. The well-signposted trail passes through a few farm gates to two pā sites. Te Mawhai pā provides views inland and is a quick diversion, while from the flat, grassy Onekawa pā site, watch the frothy trails of fishing boats traversing the ocean and imagine life during the early human occupation on this breezy headland.

MOUTOHORĀ WHALE ISLAND

Only 15 minutes offshore, this pest-free 143-hectare island is home to tuatara, North Island brown kiwi, tīeke/North Island saddleback and little blue penguins. You can explore Māori and European archaeological sites across the eroded volcanic cone, including middens/ food dumps and stone-tool manufacturing areas. Permits are needed to visit the island, but plenty of local companies whisk tourists to the island — bring togs for the hot-water beach!

KEEP AN EYE OPEN FOR
MARINE ANIMALS

Ever wondered how to tell a sea lion and fur seal apart? Sea lions have blunt noses, short whiskers and are found on or near sandy beaches. Fur seals are smaller and have pointy noses, and are often found on rocky shorelines. But always keep your distance from both!

BOTTLENOSE DOLPHIN

SHORT-BEAKED COMMON DOLPHIN

RĀPOKA
NEW ZEALAND SEA LION

KEKENO
NEW ZEALAND FUR SEAL

MAKI | ORCA
KILLER WHALE

MANGŌ TANIWHA | GREAT WHITE SHARK

ŌPŌTIKI

HUKUTAIA DOMAIN

Surviving for more than 2000 years, an ancient burial tree surrounded by a forest filled with rare and endangered plant species provides a fascinating glimpse into New Zealand's history.

INFORMATION

GRADE: Easy.

ACCESSIBILITY: Dirt paths with steps and boardwalks.

TIME: Allow 20 to 25 min return for the main loop. About 15 min for the shorter loops.

FACILITIES: Toilet. Picnic table.

LOCATION: 8 km from Ōpōtiki at 669 Woodlands Road.

DOGS: No dogs.

Stroll along well-graded dirt trails, steps and boardwalks to Taketakerau, the tapu/sacred large hollow pūriri tree used by Te Ūpokorehe iwi to safeguard the bones of their distinguished dead. View the ancient tree from all angles on the boardwalk looping beneath the over 23-metre-high gnarly native. Bones were discovered here after storm damage to the tree, and local iwi have since reburied them.

Set aside as a reserve in 1918, this dense native forest has over 80 species of trees, ferns, grasses and other introduced plants gathered from throughout New Zealand and offshore islands. King fern fronds, some nearly 3 metres long, and native trees laden with epiphytes shade trails winding through this 4.5-hectare reserve.

There are a few options to shorten the adventure, with the shortest loop having no steps. Picnic tables near the entrance are good places to watch cheeky weka darting beneath the undergrowth.

WEKA

Well known for their feisty and curious personalities, these large, brown flightless birds have a reputation for pilfering food and small objects — especially near tramping huts or farms.

They mainly eat invertebrates and fruit and have a repetitive, loud 'coo . . . et' call — often heard at dawn or within half an hour after sunset. Weka live from the coastline to above the tree line.

There are four subspecies: North Island, western, buff and Stewart Island weka.

image © Neil Robert Hutton.

ŌPŌTIKI

MOTU TRAILS DUNES TRAIL

Pedal through a unique coastal landscape on boardwalks perched above shifting dunes and past historically significant Māori sites, all within earshot of the mighty Pacific Ocean.

INFORMATION

GRADE: Grade 2 (easy).

ACCESSIBILITY: Dirt and sand trails. Boardwalks. Buggy- and wheelchair-friendly section near the western end of Elliott Street, Ōpōtiki.

TIME: Between 1 and 3 hours.

FACILITIES: Toilet and shelter at both ends.

LOCATION: The main trail begins at Memorial Park in Ōpōtiki.

DOGS: Dogs under control.

This trail provides a rare chance for cyclists and walkers to explore a fragile ecosystem, home to endangered birds such as tūturiwhatu/New Zealand dotterel, without worrying about climbs higher than 15 metres. It's peaceful and easy adventuring for all ages and abilities, with salty ocean breezes and views of bush-clad headlands meeting the Pacific Ocean.

A vast forest, including pōhutukawa, pūriri and kohekohe, once lined the coast before fire, farming, pests and land development exposed the back dunes. Local efforts to replant spinifex and pīngao/golden sand sedge are helping trap wind-blown sand, creating stable environments for regenerating shrubs and trees.

Follow little pathways to the driftwood-covered beach to take a breather, wiggle toes in the sand looking for pipi, and watch the 321-metre-high Whakaari/White Island puffing offshore. Sometimes, terehu/bottlenose dolphins and ūpokohue/pilot whales can be spotted enjoying the warm East Auckland current passing by.

ADVENTURE OPTIONS

For a quick exploration, park beside Tirohanga Beach Holiday Park on Tirohanga Road and head west for 5 minutes to the boardwalks, then east through the dunes to where Waiorua Stream spills across the beach. Bring the togs for a paddle at the beach. Afterwards, pop into Tirohanga Beach Store for ice creams. Allow 1 hour.

Alternatively, tackle the entire 10-kilometre-long (one way) trail starting at Pākōwhai ki Otutaopuku bridge over the Otara River at Memorial Park in Ōpōtiki, where there is a shelter, water fountain and toilets. Or turn around at Hukuwai (2.5 km) or Tirohanga (6 km), or where the trail goes roadside at 9 km. Allow 3 hours return.

MOTU TRAILS

This trail forms part of the Motu Trails, with short rides — including the kid-friendly Waiotahe Beach Trail — to multi-day adventures throughout the region. Find out more at motutrails.co.nz.

CENTRAL ROTORUA

KUIRAU PARK

An apocalyptic landscape surrounding a free geothermal thermal park in the centre of Rotorua is a steamy wonderland for kids to explore.

INFORMATION

GRADE: Easy.

ACCESSIBILITY: Well-graded paths. Take care around piping-hot geothermal activity.

TIME: Allow 30 min for a quick visit.

FACILITIES: Toilets available.

LOCATION: Plenty of parking on Kuirau Street.

DOGS: Dogs on leads.

Wander along paths lined with mānuka (hard-tipped leaves) and kānuka (soft-tipped leaves) past spluttering thermal vents and fenced-off mud pools leading to Kuirau Lake on the park's northern edge. The trail loops around an apocalyptic-looking lake with barren trees poking through its iridescent thermal waters.

Billowing plumes of mist often engulf the pathway beside the lake, creating fun temporary whiteouts. Ancient mātukutuku/arching clubmoss — common millions of years ago when all plants were flowerless — thrives in the warm fringes of the hot pools.

A free foot-bath at the park's southern end soothes weary adventuring feet and is also near an excellent kids' playground. Visit Kuirau Park on Saturdays for tasty fare and beverages at the local farmers' market.

TARĀPUNGA
RED-BILLED GULL

It's not often you can enjoy fish and chips at the beach without these cheeky birds watching from the sidelines, eager to finish off your tasty morsels (although takeaways and bread are not great for their tummies). These birds are kleptoparasites, which means they survive by stealing food from other animals — including humans!

It is the country's most common gull, but they are rarely found inland, except for colonies at Rotorua.

CENTRAL ROTORUA

SULPHUR BAY WILDLIFE REFUGE

If lengthier hikes don't enthuse the family, sidle around this barren slab of silica flats and sulphur ledges instead.

This wild-looking 145-hectare landscape checks off a cluster of thermal highlights, with boardwalks and trails passing close to boiling mud pools, steam vents and piping-hot mineral water.

Spy flocks of endangered birds unfazed by the acidic waters and unpredictable geothermal activity, including a colony of tarāpuka/black-billed gull that has forsaken South Island braided rivers for this moonscape. Weweia/dabchicks and pohowera/banded dotterel also live here.

Although you could explore the refuge for at least a couple of hours with Motutara Point as the turnaround point, there are plenty of highlights near the start, so it doesn't matter if the troops fancy only a short adventure.

Please keep to the boardwalks and dirt trails within the refuge to avoid disturbing the wildlife and keep safe from the scalding water.

INFORMATION

GRADE: Easy.

ACCESSIBILITY: Well-graded paths and boardwalks. Take care around geothermal activity.

TIME: Allow 30 min for a quick visit. 2 hours return to Motutara Point.

FACILITIES: Toilets available in town.

LOCATION: Multiple starting points off Hatupatu Drive behind the events centre.

DOGS: No dogs.

TARĀPUKA
BLACK-BILLED GULL

Found only in New Zealand, tarāpuka are one of the most threatened gull species in the world, with population levels rapidly declining in recent years — due to human activity, habitat loss and predation by stoats, hedgehogs, rats and cats. Tarāpuka look more 'delicate' than red-billed gulls, and breeding adults have long, thin black bills. Although they breed mainly in the South Island, there are scattered colonies at Lake Rotorua, Lake Taupō and along braided rivers in Hawke's Bay and Wairarapa.

OKERE FALLS | ROTORUA

image © Gary Clare

SH33 OKERE FALLS

OKERE FALLS

Okere River surges through a steep ravine before plummeting down a series of picturesque waterfalls — often with rafters paddling frantically in the frothy white water.

INFORMATION

GRADE: Easy.

ACCESSIBILITY: Well-graded paths and steep steps.

TIME: Allow 1 hour return.

FACILITIES: Toilets available.

LOCATION: About 20 min from Rotorua on SH33. Turn left onto Okere Falls Road.

DOGS: No dogs.

Shady pathways within the Okere Falls Scenic Reserve meander past the scattered remains of one of the nation's first hydropower stations and historic Māori sites. At the first lookout beside the turbine, watch rafters deftly navigate the half-submerged power station site and derelict machinery before walking to another lookout with views of the 7-metre-high Tutea Falls. You'll hear the terrified screams of rafters long before watching their colourful rafts plunge off the world's highest commercially rafted waterfall.

Descend Hinemoa's Steps — hand-carved in 1907 — into a dark cavern occupied by cave wētā for more views of the waterfall. Next, continue to the aptly named Trout Pools, where wily trout swim lazily against the current. From here, return the same way.

BONUS ADVENTURE

Look for the power station's original steps leading from the car park to a viewing platform alongside the fast-flowing river — very impressive after heavy rain!

TARAWERA LANDING

PUNAROMIA ROCK ART SITE

After being submerged for nearly two decades following the Tarawera eruption in 1886, these images were uncovered when Lake Tarawera receded in the early 1900s. While their age is unknown, the waka motifs drawn in kōkōwai/red ochre on rhyolite stone are surprisingly clear, despite their watery history. The art is protected under the Historic Places Act and the guardianship of the local Māori tribe, Tūhourangi.

Steps lead down to the protective grille surrounding the rock face, allowing a closer look.

INFORMATION: Allow 15 min return. From the car park, turn left at the shoreline. Toilets at the car park. Café nearby. Dogs are allowed in the car park only, not on the trail.

LOCATION: Tarawera Landing is about 17 km from Rotorua.

LAKE ŌKATAINA

TE AUHEKE TRACK/ CASCADES TRACK

During the day, this forest trail leads to the lush Cascade Falls, a 10-metre-high moss-covered cliff drenched in mini waterfalls. It's impressive for sure, but when the sun sets, it's the rather unassuming cliff face 5 minutes into the walk that lights up the forest. Thousands of twinkly glowworm 'fishing lines' dangle from the mossy rocks sheltered by lush native ferns.

Bring bug spray if planning to loiter or complete the 30-minute return walk to the Cascade Falls, as there are some aggressive little biters here.

INFORMATION: Allow 30 min to 1 hour for exploring. Cross the playing fields to the signposted trail. No dogs allowed. No toilets.

LOCATION: Located behind the Ōkataina Outdoor Education Centre on Lake Ōkataina Road.

LAKE ŌKATAINA

NGAHOPUA/TWIN LAKES TRACK

Climb steadily through native forest to vantage points above two ancient volcanic lakes, Rotongata/ Mirror Lake and Rotoatua, which formed about 35,000 years ago. Surrounded by dense podocarp forest on its steep shoreline, Rotoatua is the bigger of the two lakes. Rotongata is fringed with raupō/bulrush, providing habitat for weweia/dabchicks.

The views open along the ridgeline before the path descends and flattens out for easy walking back to Okataina Road, about 100 metres from your starting point. In winter, the trail can become muddy.

INFORMATION: Allow 1 hour (about 2 km) to complete the loop. No dogs. No toilets.

LOCATION: Park at the Ōkataina Outdoor Education Centre on Lake Ōkataina Road. Walk back to Lake Ōkataina Road, and the trailhead is directly opposite.

image © Gary Clare

LAKE TIKITAPU/BLUE LAKE

LAKE TIKITAPU NATURE WALK

Commune with nature along this short, undulating trail with information on local forest residents before taking the plunge into nearby Lake Tikitapu/Blue Lake.

INFORMATION:

GRADE: Easy.

ACCESSIBILITY: Dirt paths.

TIME: Allow 30 min return.

FACILITIES: Toilets are available at Lake Tikitapu/Blue Lake.

LOCATION: About 11 km from Rotorua, roadside parking just before Lake Tikitapu/Blue Lake on the left.

DOGS: No dogs.

Get up close to a hollow pukatea tree that survived the three peaks of Tarawera erupting in a fiery display of lightning and ash plumes in 1886 — although it didn't escape without some battle scars. Peer upwards to see epiphytic plants roosting on its branches to reach more sunshine, including a small tree alongside the ferns, supplejack and native orchids.

Native bird calls are rife within the forest; spy pīwakawaka/fantail flitting from branch to branch. Informative signs help explorers learn about local native flora and fauna while navigating the family-friendly forest trail.

Efforts are underway to boost the population of threatened native mistletoe species growing in the region. If you are very keen on mistletoe, visit the nearby 5-minute Ōkāreka Mistletoe Walk on Ōkāreka Loop Road.

LAKE TIKITAPU BLUE LAKE

Spend an hour walking through native bush and towering conifers, past secluded sandy beaches and alongside a short road section before returning to the northern shoreline of Lake Tikitapu. Take a refreshing dip or laze on grassy banks rolling down to the lake. A viewpoint on the trail near the southern shoreline has dual views of Lake Tikitapu/Blue Lake and Lake Rotokākahi/Green Lake.

Allow 1 hour to 90 min (5.5 km) for the loop. Walking only. Toilets, barbecues and playground. Dogs on leads. About 15 min from Rotorua on Tarawera Road.

LAKE ŌKĀREKA

LAKE ŌKĀREKA WALKWAY

This serene lake hasn't always been a haven for native birds stalking through tufted patches of raupō/bulrush. Things were grim 13,500 years ago, when an ancient magma chamber violently emptied itself over the neighbouring landscape, choking everything with ash. The lake formed in the subsequent depression, and until the 1960s, when an outlet was installed, water levels fluctuated wildly after rainfall.

Today, this year-round adventure is ideal for buggies for the first 2 kilometres until the boardwalk ends and the trail becomes walking only. Bring your binoculars and hunker down in the bird hide for some serious bird-twitching.

INFORMATION: Allow 90 min return for the entire 5 km (return) walk or 1 hour return for the buggy-friendly boardwalk and bird hide. No bikes or dogs.

LOCATION: Access from Acacia Road beside Lake Ōkāreka, about 15 km from Rotorua.

MOUNT NGONGOTAHĀ

NGONGOTAHĀ NATURE LOOP

Wander around an ancient volcanic dome past moss-draped trees, or take a short stroll to the viewing platform of a 40-metre-high rātā. Perch on the wooden bench and goggle at this impressive native with its whopping 1.8-metre-diameter trunk.

With more time, continue past dense tree stands with thousands of epiphytes clinging tightly. Kids can get up close to different types of fungi when the track swerves around a few decaying trees. While the path is well-groomed, the steady climb may be challenging for the smallest explorers.

INFORMATION: Allow 15 min return to the rātā or 1 hour to 90 min to stroll the 2.5-kilometre loop and avidly read all the signs. Walking only. Rustic toilet further along the trail. No dogs.

LOCATION: Parking at Violet Bonnington Reserve on Paradise Valley Road.

SH5 SOUTH ROTORUA

MAUNGA KĀKARAMEA SUMMIT TRACK

Dramatic, barren, orange and red steaming cliffs are highlights of this bike and walking trail that leads to the volcanic summit for 360-degree views. Cliffs provide a dramatic backdrop to two deep geothermal basins surrounded by the Rainbow Mountain Scenic Reserve, which has significant botanical and scientific importance – including rare plant species unique to geothermal areas.

The mountain was originally a volcano; although it has cooled, the still-smouldering landscape remains a crowd-pleaser. Regenerating kānuka provides shade while navigating the mountain's flanks.

INFORMATION: Allow 2 hours to 150 min (5 km) return. Toilets at the car park. No dogs.

LOCATION: Head south from Rotorua on SH5 for about 25 min (25 km). The car park is just after the SH38 turnoff.

WHAKAREWAREWA FOREST

REDWOOD MEMORIAL GROVE

Boardwalks over emerald-coloured thermal pools, surrounded by enormous redwoods — this is an excellent family adventure if short on time while visiting Rotorua.

INFORMATION

GRADE: Easy.

ACCESSIBILITY: Dirt paths.

TIME: Allow 30 min (2 km) for the loop.

FACILITIES: Toilets at the car park.

LOCATION: Redwoods i-SITE on Tītokorangi Drive/Longmile Road.

DOGS: Dogs on leads.

From the Redwoods visitor centre, follow red arrows into a dramatic stand of towering California redwoods, some more than 67 metres high, planted in 1901 and subsequently dedicated to the memory of New Zealand Forest Service members who died in the two world wars.

The path narrows across a boardwalk skimming the surface of colourful thermal pools, where decaying foliage and aquatic plant life float suspended in the clear water. The water clarity is remarkable, and there are plenty of places for kids to watch critters scooting across the water's surface.

Follow the sheltered undulating trail as it loops back to the car park past more giant trees — look for folks embarking on a high-ropes course beside the path. This easy outing suits all ages and provides a quick adventure in the 5600 hectare Whakarewarewa Forest.

Download an explorer trail map from the Redwoods website before visiting.

OTHER DAY-WALKS

Grab a trail map from the visitor centre for more trails, or try these family-friendly options:

WAITAWA WALK

Branching off the Memorial Grove Track, continue through stands of redwoods, Douglas fir and lush silver and mamaku ferns before returning to the car park.

INFORMATION: Allow 1 hour (3.4 km). Follow the blue markers.

QUARRY LOOKOUT TRACK

Venture further into the forest with a short climb through mature Douglas fir, European larch and various species of eucalypts to a vantage point above the old rhyolite quarry, with views across the redwood grove and city.

INFORMATION: Allow 90 min (4.8 km) return. Follow the green markers.

FIND OUT MORE
redwoods.co.nz

THE REDWOODS

WHAKAREWAREWA FOREST

Sheltered beneath the canopies of mighty trees and winding past emerald-coloured thermal lakes are about 200 kilometres of world-class biking trails for all abilities, only minutes from Rotorua's urban centre.

ROTORUA MTB CLUB

Keen local bikers formed the Rotorua MTB Club in the 1990s, and for more than three decades have been busy creating most of the trails within the forest. The club also established the RMTBC First Response Unit, which provides 24/7 medical response to people injured within the forest.

Annual memberships for individuals and families are available. Members enjoy ride nights, skills clinics and plenty of social gatherings.

FIND OUT MORE
mtbclub.org.nz

Long known as *the* destination for mountain bike riding in the central North Island, this vast forest is full of rolling berms, no-fuss trails for newbies and loops for families taking less than an hour, to more adventurous full days in the saddle. Bring the bikes or hire the latest gear from operators nearby. Take time pedalling along the sheltered trails, past geothermal hot spots, lookouts for mid-ride snacks and tempting lakes for refreshing summer dips.

WHERE TO START?

Two access points into the forest have excellent beginner ride options. Nearest to the city is Tītokorangi Drive (Longmile Road), with an information centre and toilets. Car park gates are open from 5.30am to late.

Alternatively, visit the main bike hub on Waipā State Mill Road off SH5, with rental bikes, a retail store, a café, toilets and showers. Car park gates are open from 6am to late.

FOREST INFORMATION

TRAIL GRADES: A mix of Grade 1 (easiest) through to Grade 6 (extreme).

OPENING HOURS: Riders can access the park 24 hours. However, the main car park gates are locked overnight. Check gate closure times on arrival.

ENTRANCE FEE: It's free to ride Whakarewarewa Forest. Users are encouraged to become Rotorua MTB Club members to help maintain and build new trails and support the RMTBC First Response Unit.

ARE E-BIKES ALLOWED? Yes.

ARE DOGS ALLOWED? Dogs on leads and under control.

IMPORTANT: Always follow the directional signs to avoid collisions.

EIGHT MILE ROAD
PUARENGA TRACK

This dual-use walking and biking trail weaves beneath ponga ferns and across rustic wooden bridges spanning crystal-clear spring water, and is a straightforward adventure for youngsters to find their mountain-biking mojo. Rest up on the bench seats and soak up the views. Puarenga (flowers of sulphur) refers to sulphur particles on the water's surface. Watch for walkers and families with buggies.

INFORMATION: Grade 1 (easiest). 1.4 km. Allow 30 min. Dogs on leads. Parking is available at the end of Eight Mile Road, off Waipā State Mill Road. After the vehicle gate, take the first left on to Larch Road. The trailhead is on the left.

WAIPĀ STATE MILL ROAD
WHAKAREWAREWA FOREST LOOP

Encircling the forest, the latest addition to the forest's exceptional trails takes riders past bubbling mud, thermal streams, lakes, mighty redwoods and views across stark volcanic landscapes. Mostly easy tracks and a couple of intermediate sections make it very achievable for confident kids with some miles in the saddle.

INFORMATION: Grade 1 to 3 (easiest to intermediate). 35 km. Allow 3 to 5 hours. Toilets available. Start at Te Pūtake o Tawa car park on Tarawera Road or Waipā State Mill Road off SH5.

TĪTOKORANGI DRIVE
MOKOPUNA TRACK

From the visitor centre, pedal into the forest on smooth, hard-packed gravel and dirt surfaces winding beneath the giant trees this forest is famous for. It's a dual-use trail, so watch for walkers and families with buggies. This is an ideal trail for beginner riders and returns to the visitor centre.

INFORMATION: Grade 1 (easiest). 3.2 km. Allow 30 min. Parking at Tītokorangi Drive/ Longmile Road.

WAIPĀ STATE MILL ROAD
KIDS' LITTLE LOOP

A whistlestop ride on the southern side of the forest, ideal for the youngest bikers and balance-bike riders. This short, flat dirt trail has some of the most effortless riding in the forest and passes dreamcatchers crafted from old wheel frames hanging from trees. Exit after one loop or keep going around for more miles. Follow the bright yellow signs about 20 metres down the main trail.

INFORMATION: Grade 1 (easiest). 400 m. Allow 10 min. Parking at Waipā State Mill Road off SH5.

WAIPĀ STATE MILL ROAD
KIDS' LOOP

This longer loop combines the Kids' Little Loop, Tahi and Dipper tracks for an epic hour or so in the saddle. Some nice flowy downhill sections with excellent variety and a final section winding between girthy redwood trees. If the kids tire, there are plenty of exit points back to the car park to shorten the ride. Follow the bright yellow signs about 20 metres down the main trail.

INFORMATION: Grade 2 (easy). 4.5 km. Allow about 45 min to 1 hour. Parking at Waipā State Mill Road off SH5.

SH5 TOWARDS TAUPŌ

WAIOTAPU BOARDWALK

Perched on the edge of a mud pool, this boardwalk provides plenty of angles to watch the burping landscape release eggy-scented gases. Take a short walk to the upper viewing platform to peer over the 45-metre-wide mud field, which could be more than a few thousand years old. It's not the biggest mud pool in the Bay of Plenty, but it's free, fun and gets everyone close to the action. If the science of mud appeals, the interpretation panels are worth reading.

INFORMATION: Allow 10 min return. Suitable for walking, buggies and wheelchairs on the boardwalk; walking only to the upper viewpoint. No dogs allowed.

LOCATION: Head south from Rotorua on SH5 for about 30 min (30 km). Turn left onto Waiotapu Loop Road and follow the mud pool signs.

SH5 TOWARDS TAUPŌ

KEROSENE CREEK

These bush- and fern-shrouded hot pools are no longer a locals' secret. The creek's inclusion in popular tourist guides means there is a fair chance you'll eavesdrop on a few different nationalities here. But despite its popularity, this steamy waterfall still offers enjoyable toe-warming opportunities and wallowing spots for families. Arrive early for a more sedate soaking experience. From the car park, walk beside the stream to the dirt trail leading to the main waterfall and swimming hole. Due to its natural source, putting your head underwater is not recommended.

INFORMATION: Suitable for walking only. Allow 30 min return — more for bathing. No dogs. Toilet at the car park. Check gate closures on arrival.

LOCATION: Drive from Rotorua towards Taupō on SH5 for about 25 min (26 km). Turn left onto Old Waiotapu Road and follow the 1-kilometre-long gravel road.

SH5 TOWARDS TAUPŌ

TE KOPIA WALK

This little-known geothermal field doesn't draw the crowds like some crowded Rotorua attractions. Still, it's an excellent detour for its multiple aqua-coloured pools with a backdrop of exposed red banks on the towering Paeroa Range.

From the car park, follow the fenceline to the first vantage point before climbing the stairs onto the boardwalk leading into the Te Kopia geothermal field past rare and endangered prostrate kānuka. A viewing platform between the pools lets you peer into the geothermal activity. Because water levels fluctuate, you'll spy either active squirting mud or brightly coloured geothermal lakes.

INFORMATION: Walking only. Allow 20 min return. 200 metres one way. No facilities. No dogs.

LOCATION: At Waiotapu, turn off SH5 onto Waikite Valley Road for 9.3 km, then Te Kopia Road — the trail starts about 8.5 km along the road. Parking beside the road.

RELAX AND LOOK UP

WHAT CLOUD IS THAT?

Clouds are made up of tiny water droplets and ice crystals, which are super small and can float in the air. When the droplets get large enough, you can see them as cloud or fog. If they become even larger, they can turn into rain or snow.

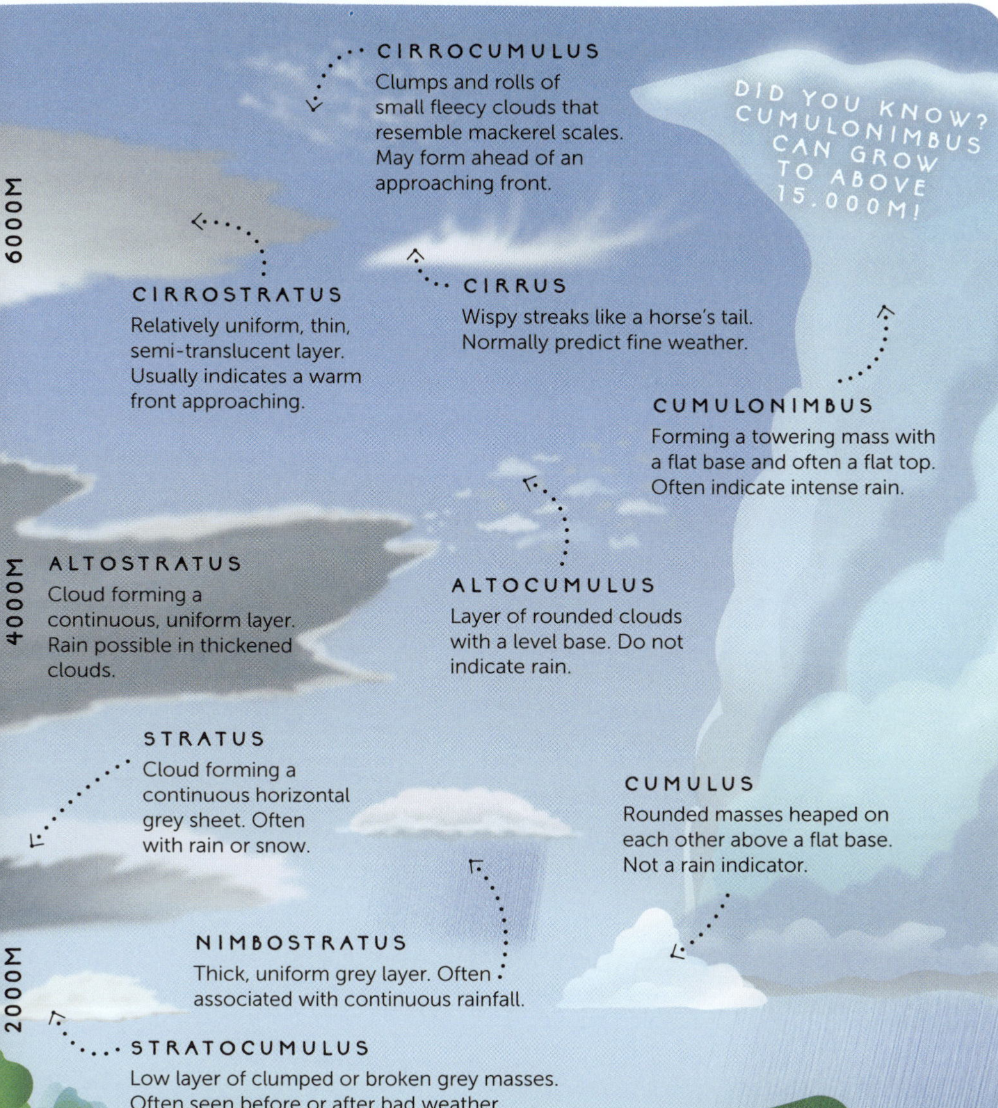

EXPLORE THE

CENTRE OF THE NORTH ISLAND

Looming large over the eruption-battered Central Plateau, a trio of brooding volcanoes dominate the horizon while cascading icy-blue waters erode ancient lava flows, and pathways meander beneath giant native trees saved by eco-warriors.

HIGHLIGHTS

REFLECTIONS OF MOUNT RUAPEHU IN ALPINE BOGS FILLED WITH CARNIVOROUS SUNDEWS

Stroll along an alpine boardwalk to Tongariro National Park's highest waterfall, the picturesque tiered Waitonga Falls, before picnicking and exploring near its base (p167).

A MILD STREAM TRANSFORMS INTO A RAGING RIVER SURGING THROUGH A NARROW CHASM

Time a visit with the opening of the Aratiatia Dam gates for a crowd-pleasing wild frothy display near Taupō (p141).

WALK THROUGH VIRGIN NATIVE BUSH TO A FOREST-SHROUDED LAGOON

Watch dragonflies hover above the sparkling clear waters of Ohinetonga Lagoon (p162) before taking a refreshing dip in the Whakapapa River.

HUKA FALLS ROAD
HUKA FALLS

Watch as the Waikato River squeezes through a narrow rock chasm before splaying into turbulent whirlpools in a spectacular display of nature's power and beauty. A year-round crowd-pleaser.

INFORMATION

GRADE: Easy.

ACCESSIBILITY: Well-graded concrete and dirt paths suitable for buggies and wheelchairs.

TIME: Allow 20 min (400 m) return.

FACILITIES: No facilities.

LOCATION: Drive north from Taupō on Wairākei Drive. Turn right onto Huka Falls Road (well signposted). Check gate-closure times on arrival.

DOGS: On leads.

Created by thousands of years of erosion, this bottleneck blasts nearly a quarter of a million litres of sparkling blue water every second along a series of small waterfalls before a final 11-metre-high plunge into churning waters. Marvel at the frothy action from various lookouts; peer over the footbridge near the car park, where the Waikato River narrows from about 100 metres wide to a snug 15 metres, before continuing to the main lookout beside the thundering falls. Beyond, the swift-moving waters settle and continue sedately downstream, ultimately to the Tasman Sea. Get closer to the action with a jet boat ride or river cruise to experience the fall's spray while bouncing across the foam.

HIDDEN TRAIL

A little-known walking trail that arguably gives better, uncrowded views of the falls (top image) begins from the northern edge of the car park. Follow the unmarked path for less than a minute to a downstream vantage point where the occasional brave kayaker can be seen hurtling over the waterfall.

GEOLOGY

Beneath the falls is a layer of rock called the Huka Falls Formation, created when deep sediment deposits sank to the bottom of an ancient lake 70,000 to 200,000 years ago and hardened like natural concrete. Over time, erosion has carved into the layer, creating a rock-bound chasm for the Waikato River to squeeze through.

SH5 NAPIER–TAUPŌ HIGHWAY

ŌPEPE NORTHERN LOOP

This short adventure close to Taupō is all about enormous trees to peer up into and clamber over, some with trunks with dark holes to climb through — if the kids feel brave.

INFORMATION

GRADE: Easy.

ACCESSIBILITY: Well-graded dirt paths.

TIME: Allow 30 to 45 min (1.5 km) for the loop.

FACILITIES: None.

LOCATION: Ōpepe Scenic and Historic Reserve is 17 km from Taupō on SH5 (Napier–Taupō Highway).

DOGS: On leads.

This ancient, wizened podocarp forest shades an undulating trail that quickly whisks adventurers away from the busy highway into its serene leafy reserve. Many of these mighty natives also survived extensive fires and logging. Take time to ogle at their vast, sometimes weatherbeaten canopies far above while exploring the forest loop. Helpful signage adds an educational element to the outing.

The reserve is home to a nearly 30-metre-high rimu with a girth of 6.6 metres, which has deservedly been added to the New Zealand Tree Register.

HISTORY

In its heyday, the Ōpepe township boasted a hotel, a store and homes for 120 residents. It was also the scene of a one-sided skirmish between European militia and Māori in June 1869. Nine Bay of Plenty Cavalry members were killed when a band of warriors led by prophet and guerrilla leader Te Kooti (founder of the Ringatū Church) attacked their camp. Trooper George Crosswell, who had been drying his rain-drenched uniform, managed to escape and travel naked across 64 kilometres of rough country to report the attack. A short, 5-minute side trail leads to a small cemetery that includes the graves of the British soldiers.

LONGER ADVENTURE

Further explore the reserve along the southern walking track through regenerating forest, on the other side of SH5, which takes about 1 hour to 90 minutes (3 km) to complete. Highlights include a saw pit (20 min return) and relics from the historic settlement.

SPA THERMAL PARK

OTUMUHEKE STREAM

Wallow in steamy natural pools created by the colliding waters of the thermal Otumuheke Stream and chilly Waikato River.

INFORMATION

GRADE: Easy.

ACCESSIBILITY: Well-graded concrete and dirt paths suitable for buggies and bikes.

TIME: Allow 10 min one way walking to the stream.

FACILITIES: Toilet, coffee kiosk and changing facilities available.

LOCATION: Follow the signs downhill from Spa Thermal Park car park on Country Avenue off Spa Road. Plenty of parking but check gate closure times on arrival.

DOGS: On leads.

Once a rustic gem, the boulder-strewn mouth of Otumuheke Stream has become a lively destination for locals and tourists to find their perfect 'natural hot tub' where the thermal stream mingles with New Zealand's longest river.

Sandwiched between the rolling hills of Spa Thermal Park and the 425-kilometre-long Waikato River, the wallowing hole has undergone a significant streamside refurbishment, including toilets, a coffee kiosk and changing facilities. As a result, it is firmly on the tourist circuit.

Avoid the masses and sometimes rowdy evening crowd by visiting earlier in the day. Non-toe-dipping visitors can lounge on wooden platforms overlooking the steamy natural wonder.

The hot stream is 1.5 kilometres long, and historically local Māori used this area for sacred healing.

TAKE A DIP ABOVE A SUPERVOLCANO

Beneath the sparkling waters of Lake Taupō lurks a supervolcano. Its most recent eruption 1800 years ago was a colossal, violent event that spewed significant debris into the atmosphere — reportedly turning the sky blood-red as far away as Rome and blackening skies in China.

Known as the Hatepe eruption, the catastrophic explosion devastated large swathes of land across the North Island with fast-moving pyroclastic flows (hot gas and volcanic matter) charring the landscape at speeds of between 600 and 900 kilometres per hour. Pumice and ash filled many of the island's major river valleys, and pumice remains plentiful, bobbing on Lake Taupō's shallow shoreline. It is considered New Zealand's largest eruption in the past 20,000 years. Covering 616 square kilometres, the lake is 46 kilometres long and has a maximum depth of 186 metres.

COUNTRY ROAD

SPA THERMAL PARK TO HUKA FALLS

Connecting two Taupō highlights, the riverside trail from Spa Thermal Park rises high on cliffs overlooking the mighty Waikato River on its way to the even mightier Huka Falls.

INFORMATION

GRADE: Easy.

ACCESSIBILITY: Short section of concrete but mainly well-graded dirt paths.

TIME: Allow about 45 min to 1 hour (3 km one way) each way.

FACILITIES: Toilets at Spa Thermal Park.

LOCATION: Spa Thermal Park on Country Road off Spa Road.

DOGS: On leads.

From the car park, follow the trail past sprawling grassy banks to Otumuheke Stream (p138). Beyond, the trail continues downstream on a wide, undulating dirt path that rises to vantage points offering bird's-eye views of tiny shrubby islands and dramatic rock bluffs. A wooden viewing platform about halfway along provides an opportunity to refuel and rest up.

The trail flattens beside the swift-moving Waikato River as it begins to narrow near Huka Falls. The thundering falls can be heard before the river squeezes through a narrow 15-metre-wide bottleneck and erupts into an 11-metre-high waterfall.

Either return the same way or arrange transport from Huka Falls car park. The path is doable with buggies, although a few steep sections will give the arms a hefty workout.

IMPORTANT

Keep an eye on kids near the exposed high points. Swimming in the swift currents of the Waikato River is highly discouraged. No bikes allowed. Intermediate (Grade 3) bikers can use the nearby Rotary Ride (p146).

ARATIATIA RAPIDS | SH5

SH5 ROTORUA–TAUPŌ HIGHWAY

ARATIATIA RAPIDS

Within minutes a middling stream transforms into a thundering river surging through remnants of an ancient volcano.

INFORMATION

GRADE: Easy.

ACCESSIBILITY: Mix of concrete (by bridge) and dirt paths with steps (to lookouts). Buggy- and wheelchair-friendly by the bridge.

TIME: Bridge Viewpoint is beside the car park, Mid Viewpoint 5 min (250 m) and Top Viewpoint 10 min (350 m).

FACILITIES: Toilet.

LOCATION: North of the Wairākei roundabout, turn off SH5 onto Aratiatia Road. Plenty of parking beside the dam.

DOGS: On leads.

Arrive on time to experience the blaring sirens and see the dam gates open before the unleashed Waikato River fills a narrow, rocky gorge. From the dam gates, the turquoise waters rapidly fall 28 metres over 1 kilometre, and all the crowd-pleasing action is viewable from three easily accessible lookouts.

For all the highlights, begin on the bridge, and after the dam gates open, promptly trot to the well-signposted downstream clifftop Mid Viewpoint to watch the show play out — plenty of time to do both if moving briskly. Or, if time is tight, choose either vantage point —both are worthwhile.

Folks with more time can view the surging of 80,000 litres of water per second from another angle if they stroll further along to the Top Viewpoint (recommended only if the legs need stretching).

Since 1964, the Aratiatia Power Station has harnessed the Waikato River above the rapids for hydroelectric power generation. Timed releases are purely for show, to give visitors a glimpse of how the rapids would have once looked.

Lord of the Rings fans will recognise the rapids from a scene in *The Hobbit: The Desolation of Smaug,* when the dwarves escaped downriver in barrels. For two days, during each release, the film crew dropped about 25 empty barrels into the water to capture the raw footage required.

IMPORTANT

The rapids are NEVER safe to swim in, as the dam can release water any time and without warning.

GATE RELEASE TIMES

April to September: 10am, 12pm, 2pm. October to March: 10am, 12pm, 2pm and 4pm.

WAIPĀHĪHĪ

WAIPĀHĪHĪ BOTANICAL GARDENS

Recharge the family's batteries at a hilltop reserve that explodes in a mass of colourful flowers in springtime.

Even outside the vibrant flowering period during October and November, visiting with a picnic to soak up the lake and volcanic peaks views is still an excellent outing for the troops. A tangled network of trails zigzag through the different collections of rare alpine plants, rhododendrons and camellias.

Keep an eye out for painted Taupō Rocks, seemingly hidden on every trail corner and tree-trunk nook, and listen to the birdsong returning to the forest remnant.

Short on time or feeling unmotivated to walk? Drive the 2-kilometre loop winding through the gardens lined with towering stands of native trees and ferns.

From the car park, choose from any of the trails marked on the welcome map.

HANDY HINT

Snap a photo of the welcome map to navigate the many pathways.

INFORMATION

GRADE: Easy.

ACCESSIBILITY: Gravel, dirt and concrete paths. Bikes are allowed on the road loop but not within the forest.

TIME: Allow 1 hour for a free-range exploration.

FACILITIES: Toilet beside the car park.

LOCATION: Corner of Hyde Avenue and Shepherd Road, Waipāhīhī. Check gate closure times on arrival.

DOGS: On leads.

ACACIA BAY

RANGATIRA POINT TRACK

The smooth, flat volcanic rock ledges at Whakamoenga Point provide launching pads for manu bombs or sedate picnics overlooking the tranquil shoreline.

INFORMATION

GRADE: Easy.

ACCESSIBILITY: Well-graded dirt paths.

TIME: Allow 30 min one way to Whakamoenga Point.

FACILITIES: None.

LOCATION: Follow Acacia Bay Road to the end. Parking is available before the private road sign.

DOGS: On leads.

Follow along the eroded shoreline and fern-clad small rocky coves past brightly coloured rowboats on a well-maintained trail. Roots occasionally splay across the dirt path and lichen-covered rocks emerge from the ground, making this a walking-only adventure.

About halfway along, follow the well-signposted public access near the concrete jetty before entering the bush again. Narrowing across a small headland, the trail passes a sizeable rocky cave where moa bones were discovered. Rock walls with spindly trees teetering above line the path to the first access point, where a lava flow juts into the lake. A second access point has more impressive views of the strange hummocky landscape created as the lava cooled, with plenty of space for grabbing a bite. Pumice whips around in eddies near little rock canals where the swelling water makes booming echoes. Remember to slip, slop, slap and wrap, as neither outcrop provides shade.

Anglers can dangle a line, hopefully snaring a trout for dinner, although fishing licences are required. Sailing boats and kayaks often glide past towards the nearby famous 14-metre-high Ngātoroirangi/Mine Bay rock carvings by master carver Matahi Whakataka-Brightwell — although they are not visible from the point. Instead, enjoy views of the volcanic peaks of Tongariro National Park dominating the horizon, or plunge into the sparkling waters of Lake Taupō before returning the same way.

SH5 NAPIER–TAUPŌ

MOUNT TAUHARA

For folks keen on clambering up a mountain on trails winding beneath native forest to dramatic vistas across volcanic landscapes and views of Lake Taupō, don't miss hiking up this 65,000-year-old dormant volcano. Join the steady stream of locals and tourists navigating steep pasture for 20 minutes before entering the forest and embarking on a steady climb, often with rooty sections and through narrow dirt channels. Closer to the summit, there is some respite on more undulating terrain before the final push to the trig at 1088 metres above sea level. But don't stop at the trig. Instead, follow the path to the exposed rocky outcrop for swoon-worthy views of the Central Plateau. Be prepared for chilly, windy conditions at the top.

INFORMATION: Dirt trail with steps, at times rough. Walking only. Allow 2 to 3 hours return. Stiles to cross. No facilities. No dogs.

LOCATION: 10 min from town on Mountain Road off SH5 Napier–Taupō Highway. Plenty of parking.

SH5 NAPIER–TAUPŌ

KAIMANAWA WALL

These are possibly some of the most unusual rocks you can easily access in New Zealand. The mysteriously rectangular rock blocks have sparked wide-ranging debate since being discovered; are they from a pre-Māori civilisation, a megalithic 'power node' or perhaps an ancient temple of learning? While various creative theories abound, geologists have visited and concluded that natural fractures in the 330,000-year-old volcanic ignimbrite rock created the block shapes. The winding drive to the wall through the beech forest is beautiful year-round.

INFORMATION: Viewable from the road. Limited roadside parking. No facilities. No dogs.

LOCATION: 28 km east of Taupō on SH5, turn onto Taharua Road, then Clements Mill Road through Kaimanawa Forest Park. The wall is almost precisely 12 km on the left.

TAUPŌ TOWNSHIP

TONGARIRO DOMAIN PLAYGROUND AND MINIATURE TRAIN

Kids can defy gravity on the towering spider net before swooping down the slide, splash about in the water-play area or choose from smaller activities dotted around the playground. Little kids even have a dedicated mini-playground.

Jump on the Lions Club Express train for an enjoyable tootle around the southern part of the park on public and school holidays (during summer, it runs every weekend). With its bright red carriages, this iconic railway has entertained train buffs for decades.

INFORMATION: Toilets and drinking fountains at the domain. Ice cream parlours nearby on Tongariro Street. The train is weather dependent and costs $2 per ride. Covered shoes are required. No dogs.

LOCATION: Parking is available on Story Place or Ferry Road on the lakefront.

image © Love Taupō

EXPLORE ON TWO WHEELS

TAUPŌ BIKE ADVENTURES

Taupō is home to plenty of family-friendly bike trails, so jump in the saddle and tootle alongside the turquoise waters of Lake Taupō, bike to the mighty Huka Falls or tackle the adventurous Great Lake Trail. For maps and more information, visit biketaupo.org.nz.

CENTRAL TAUPŌ

GREAT LAKE PATHWAY/ LIONS WALK

Voted one of the nation's best urban rides, the Great Lake Pathway is bike riding at its easiest. Beginning from the Taupō Boat Harbour, the shared pathway hugs the lake's edge before ending at Waitahanui. Cool off by taking a dip in the many secluded bays the trail passes. Most of the 10-kilometre-long trail is concrete, making it ideal for young riders. It's an out-and-back pathway, so bike for as long as the family remains enthusiastic.

GRADE: Grade 1 (easiest).

ACCESSIBILITY: Dirt and concrete paths suitable for buggies, bikes and wheelchairs.

TIME: 1 to 3 hours return.

DISTANCE: 10 km one way or as short as needed.

FACILITIES: Toilets, playgrounds and drinking fountains along the way.

LOCATION: Start at Taupō Boat Harbour; plenty of parking on Lake Terrace.

DOGS: On leads.

image © Love Taupō

SPA THERMAL PARK

THE ROTARY RIDE

This undulating trail loosely follows the Waikato River north towards Huka Falls as it climbs through native bush onto a ridge, before passing beneath towering pine trees. Then, navigate gullies and soak up views of the river far below before a gradual descent. Choose to ride back for a soak at the thermal Otumuheke Stream (p138) or cross the Waikato River to ride the trails alongside Wairākei Drive back into town.

GRADE: Grade 3 (intermediate).

ACCESSIBILITY: Dirt and concrete paths suitable for biking and walking only.

TIME: 45 min one way.

DISTANCE: 5.5 km one way.

FACILITIES: Toilets at Spa Thermal Park.

LOCATION: Begin at either Spa Thermal Park or Huka Falls car park.

DOGS: On leads.

SPA THERMAL PARK

RIVERSIDE TRAIL

Beginning beside the Control Gates Bridge near the town, this trail passes through the grassy Riverbank Reserve before narrowing towards the former café and animal attraction on Cherry Island. Nearby, perch on the grassy rolling hill and admire the Waikato River flowing beside vast exposed bluffs before climbing to Spa Road, where folks plunge themselves off the bungy platform. Then, it's easy cycling into Spa Thermal Park. Extend the adventure by completing the Rotary Ride (see left).

GRADE: Grade 3 (intermediate).

ACCESSIBILITY: Dirt and concrete paths not suitable for buggies.

TIME: 15 min one way.

DISTANCE: 3 km one way.

FACILITIES: Toilets at Spa Thermal Park or in town.

LOCATION: Begin at either Spa Thermal Park or a car park at Gates Park near the Control Gates Bridge (accessible only when travelling south).

DOGS: On leads.

image © Love Taupō

IDENTIFY NATIVE BIRDS

Keep your ears open and eyes peeled for these birds that call New Zealand home.

1. PĪWAKAWAKA FANTAIL

Take a peek behind you while exploring because these friendly birds often follow along checking the disturbed soil for tasty bugs. Listen out for their friendly 'cheet cheet', and hopefully they'll put on a very energetic flying display for you. Look for their distinctive fanned tail as they dart around. They are known for being quite vocal, except when it is particularly cold.

2. KERERŪ | NEW ZEALAND PIGEON

These big birds are very quiet except when they crash-land in the trees! Only occasionally will you hear them let loose a soft 'oo'. Importantly, they spread the seed of more than 70 native forest plants. They are widespread throughout New Zealand and on some forested/ shrubby offshore islands.

3. TŪĪ | PARSON BIRD

Tūī enjoy feasting on nectar but when that is scarce they feed on fruit and insects. Around September and October, you may see them diving and duet singing when they're courting their mate. Tūī are found nowhere else in the world.

4.PŌPOKOTEA WHITEHEAD

Found in flocks high in the forest canopy, where they are on the hunt for spiders, moths and beetles. They can often be seen hanging upside down while feeding! Their tuneful calls are common in North Island beech forests, podocarp forest and old-growth exotic plantation forests. They are about 15 centimetres long and have black beaks and eyes.

5. MIROMIRO | TOMTIT

These small birds are about 13 centimetres long and weigh only 11 grams. The oldest known miromiro was 16 years old, which is impressive because the average life expectancy is only three years. Look out for their bulky nests in tree forks. Tomtits often perch on a branch or cling to a trunk while scanning for prey, before swiftly flying down to snatch it.

6. KŌTARE | SACRED KINGFISHER

These unique birds are often spotted in elevated spots, including the tops of fence posts or telephone wires, which lets them spy on their dinner. Their calls are rather unmusical! They use their bill to chisel out nests in cliffs, banks and cuttings. Near estuaries they mainly eat small crabs, while in open country they munch on cicadas, beetles, wētā, small lizards and mice.

ADVENTUROUS RIDES

GREAT LAKE TRAIL

When the family is ready to conquer some smooth-flowing intermediate trails, take a journey around the rim of a supervolcano on the Great Lake Trail. Three epic sections can be ridden over three days or mix it up with half-day adventures (p149). These Grade 3 trails along the lake's northwestern shoreline are best saved for when the family is more experienced, as some sections navigate relatively remote — but spectacular! — areas. For detailed trail maps, transport options and more information, visit greatlaketrail.com.

WAIHĀHĀ SECTION

Begin beside the Waihāhā River before a gentle climb high onto cliffs above a bush-clad gorge dominated by tānekaha/celery pine. Enjoy scenic views of the volcanic landscape before descending on flowing single-trails, with bridges, platforms and boardwalks, past clifftop lookouts and the mysterious Echo Rock to Kotukutuku Landing at Waihora Bay. Take a refreshing dip in the turquoise waters of Lake Taupō while waiting for pre-arranged boat transport to Kinloch village, where the troops can be refuelled. Keen, fit riders can make it an out-and-back ride.

INFORMATION: Grade 3 (intermediate). 4 to 5 hours (30 km) one way plus boat trip. Waihāhā River car park off SH32, 50-min drive from Taupō.

image © Sarah Bennett

KAWAKAWA SECTION

Combining the Ōrākau, K2K and Otaketake trails into one spectacular loop, this section begins at Kinloch and takes in flowing downhill single-track descents through regenerating forest and harakeke/flax wetlands, climbing to vantage points where the reward is majestic views of Lake Taupō. Pedal over boardwalks and ravines to the shoreline of Lake Taupō at Kawakawa Bay, where you can stay the night at the campsite if bike-packing, or have a well-deserved swim before leaving the sparkling bay behind to continue your journey. Ride either clockwise or anti-clockwise.

INFORMATION: Grade 3 (intermediate). 4 to 5 hours (32 km) for the entire loop. Kinloch village, 20-min drive from Taupō.

image © Brendon Burchell

WHAKAIPO SECTION

This section can be ridden in either direction, but is often started in Kinloch where you leave the marina behind to climb steadily through native bush onto the headland. Here, the optional Headland Loop sweeps across bluffs to impressive vantage points that look across the lake to Tongariro National Park and the Kaimanawa Ranges. The loop reconnects to the main trail for a fast, flowing descent into popular Whakaipo Bay. Enjoy a dip or snacks to refuel, then return the same way or arrange land/boat transfers back to Kinloch or Taupō.

INFORMATION: Grade 3 (intermediate). 1.5 to 2 hours (13 km) one way. Add 1 hour for the 9.5 km Headland Loop. Kinloch village, 20-min drive from Taupō. Or Whakaipo Bay, 15 min drive from Taupō.

GREAT LAKE TRAIL

ŌRĀKAU TRAIL

Winding gently down to the glistening shoreline of Lake Taupō, past wetlands and through bush-clad valleys, this trail is considered the easiest of the Great Lake Trail sections. From the car park, there's smooth riding on soft pine needles beneath towering pine trees before a moss-lined trail continues its descent towards the lake, crossing wooden bridges spanning narrow, deep ravines.

At Kawakawa Bay, emerge onto a small, secluded pebble beach. Bring the togs for a refreshing dip with the mighty volcanic peaks of Tongariro National Park on the horizon. Return the way you came, or pre-book a water taxi to whisk everyone to Kinloch.

INFORMATION: Grade 3 (intermediate). Allow 1 to 1.5 hours (10.25 km) one way. Dogs under control.

LOCATION: The well-signposted Ōrākau Trail car park on Whangamata Road is 27 km from Taupō and 10 km from Kinloch.

GREAT LAKE TRAIL

OTAKETAKE TRAIL

Pedal alongside a quiet country road before disappearing beneath native forest as the trail traverses a gorge high above Whangamata Road. Descending from its lofty beginnings on the side of the forested gorge, the trail turns south towards Lake Taupō and navigates small gullies and the occasional switchback — younger kids may need to push their bikes here. Take a snack break or catch your breath from the lookouts with views of Otaketake Stream winding through the deep valley, and across Kinloch to Mount Tauhara. Once you reach the Kawakawa to Kinloch (K2K) junction, there are 3 kilometres of easy homeward-bound pedalling following high above, then alongside the shoreline.

INFORMATION: Grade 3 (intermediate). Allow 1.5 to 2.5 hours (12 km) one way. Dogs under control.

LOCATION: The well-signposted Ōrākau Trail car park on Whangamata Road is 27 km from Taupō and 10 km from Kinloch.

GREAT LAKE TRAIL

W2K LOOKOUT

From Kinloch Marina, follow the signs past Kinloch Domain, where the trail winds between mammoth moss-covered boulders towards Boojum Dell. Then it's a steep climb beneath the native forest, with some sharp dips and switchbacks for the first couple of kilometres before the trail levels off and becomes more undulating. At the Headland Loop junction, turn right and follow the Kinloch Lookout signs to a vantage spot above Whangamata Bay. Refuel and take in views of Te Kauwae Point's jagged exposed bluffs, remnants of the lake's volcanic past, Pureora Forest Park, and boats leaving Kinloch marina to catch trout lurking in the vast volcanic caldera.

INFORMATION: Grade 3 (intermediate). Allow 1 to 1.5 hours (about 7.5 km) one way. Dogs under control.

LOCATION: Parking is available near the shelter on Mata Place opposite the Kinloch marina. Kinloch is 20 km from Taupō.

NORTH TAUPŌ

CRATERS MTB PARK

This purpose-built mountain bike park only 10 minutes north of Taupō has kilometres of single-track trails to explore for an hour up to a full day.

Saddle up for adventures within a sprawling pine and eucalyptus plantation that is rideable year-round due to its free-draining volcanic pumice soils. Grab a visitor pass or a Bike Taupō annual membership and tackle sedate beginner trails to more technical routes for experienced riders.

WHERE TO START?

Scraggs Out is an excellent easy (Grade 2) option for riders with its smooth-flowing dirt berms and optional humped wooden boardwalks. The trailhead is beneath the overbridge at the Karapiti Road car park, and the 1-kilometre-long single-track trail ends after Scraggs Tunnel beside Manager's Corner. Then turn left and follow the easy 4WD Powerline Road for about 500 metres back to the car park.

The easy (Grade 2) Kids' Track is a fun, short dirt trail suiting young riders. From the Karapiti Road car park, cross the footbridge and follow the signs. The trail connects with the Tourist Trap trail, making it about a 630-metre-long loop.

BIKE TAUPŌ

Get among the action by joining Bike Taupō. Annual individual, family and visitor passes are available online or at local cycle shops.

Kids Bike Taupō meets every Thursday at the Karapiti Road car park between 3.30 and 5.00pm. The sessions are ideal for families unfamiliar with the area who would like a friendly introduction. Please bring sensible biking clothes, enclosed shoes and water.

FIND OUT MORE
bikeTaupo.org.nz

INFORMATION

WHAT FACILITIES ARE AT KARAPITI ROAD CAR PARK? Toilets, park map and shelter.

WHAT GRADES ARE THE TRAIL? A mix of Grade 2 (easy) to Grades 4–5 (technical).

WHEN IS THE PARK OPEN? The trails are accessible 24/7.

HOW MUCH DOES IT COST TO RIDE IN THE PARK? All users must be members of Bike Taupō or purchase a visitor pass.

ARE E-BIKES ALLOWED ON THE TRAIL? Pedal-assist e-bikes are welcome.

ARE DOGS ALLOWED ON THE TRAIL? Yes, but they must be kept under control.

IMPORTANT: Always remember to slip, slop, slap and wrap. Bring plenty of water and snacks.

LOCATION: Multiple entrances, but a good starting point is the Karapiti Road car park off Wairākei Drive, about 3 kilometres north of Taupō.

KINLOCH

WHANGAMATA STREAM TRAIL

With wide, flat forest trails, a fairy-house glade and the clear waters of Lake Taupō for an after-ride dip, this family-friendly adventure makes an excellent half-day outing.

INFORMATION

GRADE: Easy.

ACCESSIBILITY: Well-graded dirt trail and wooden bridges.

TIME: Allow 1 hour return (about 7 km) biking.

FACILITIES: Toilets at Kinloch village.

LOCATION: Plenty of parking near Kinloch beach, 20 km from Taupō.

DOGS: On leads.

From Kinloch, ride west along the shoreline of Lake Taupō to the well-signposted turnoff before turning inland to connect with the winding Whangamata Stream. The trails suit all abilities and are wide and forgiving for wobbly youngsters still mastering two wheels.

Take a breather at the water wheel, a replica of one installed in the 1950s to pump water to a nearby woolshed on the original Whangamata Station. Then pedal beneath stands of larch, Douglas fir, Tasmanian blackwood, apple trees, oak and beech. Once a barren farm, the area has become a local success story, with volunteers planting trees and eradicating weeds since the 1970s to create a haven for native birds.

Just before the trail ends at Whangamata Road, follow signs to the Loop Walk Cross Bridge, where trout sometimes hide beneath the overhanging banks of the Whangamata Stream or mill about in the clear water. Between April and November, this is an important spawning stream for brown and

rainbow trout, which form 'redds' or shallow depressions in the gravel to lay and fertilise their eggs.

A short detour takes older kids over a humpy MTB trail before the vast fairy glade filled with whimsical creations, before the trail continues back to the shoreline.

SH47 TŪRANGI TO NATIONAL PARK

TE PŌRERE REDOUBT

In the shadow of Mount Tongariro, these two impressive British-style redoubts were the site of the last major battle of the New Zealand Wars, in the 1860s.

On 4 October 1869, a bloody conflict erupted between the followers of Māori leader and guerrilla fighter Te Kooti Arikirangi Te Tūruki and more than 500 British soldiers and their Māori allies. Te Kooti fought alongside Ngāti Tūwharetoa and faced government forces who were armed with rifles and heavy artillery. By the end of the day, 41 people had died, but Te Kooti evaded the government soldiers. Although he escaped with his life, he lost two fingers on his left hand.

From the car park, look for endangered whio/blue ducks camouflaged on rocks beside the clear, flowing stream and listen for the male's distinctive 'whio' whistle. Then follow the easy gravel trail to the first redoubt's viewing platform, before continuing on a steady 10-minute climb along gravel paths with steps to the second, larger redoubt.

IMPORTANT

Te Pōrere is a wāhi tapu/sacred site. Climbing on the lower redoubt walls isn't permitted; please use the trenches. The upper redoubt is an urupā/cemetery so please respect the area, and view the redoubt from the tower only.

ON THE WAY

The scenic lookout halfway along Te Ponanga Saddle Road from Tūrangi is worth a detour for panoramic views across Lake Taupō and Maunganamu/Mosquito Hill, encircled by the Tokaanu Tailrace Canal.

INFORMATION

GRADE: Easy.

ACCESSIBILITY: Well-graded dirt and gravel trail with steps.

TIME: Allow 40 min return.

FACILITIES: None.

LOCATION: The signposted car park on SH47 is near the junction with SH46, 26 km from Tūrangi.

DOGS: No dogs.

TOKAANU

TOKAANU THERMAL WALK

Discover spluttering mud and crystal-clear thermal pools on a short walk through an active volcanic landscape.

INFORMATION

GRADE: Easy.

ACCESSIBILITY: Well-graded gravel path suitable for buggies and assisted wheelchair users. The trail passes near exposed boiling mud and thermal water pools.

TIME: Allow 20 min for the loop.

FACILITIES: None.

LOCATION: Mangaroa Street, Tokaanu, SH41. The trailhead is beside the thermal pool complex.

DOGS: No dogs.

Amuse young adventurers with bubbling, farting mud emitted by deep volcanic forces along a wide, flat trail. Sidling beneath regenerating native bush and through a landscape pockmarked with thermal vents, the buggy- and wheelchair-friendly trail passes deep, sparkly pools and splattering mud. Boardwalks and viewing platforms provide vantage points of sinter basins, where overflowing hot springs have created flat and mounded rock areas from very fine-grained silica.

Since the sixteenth century, Ngāti Kurauia have lived alongside the Tokaanu Stream, using the hot water and steam vents for communal cooking, dyeing clothing and therapeutic bathing. Later, the thermal waters were also a popular rest-stop for coaches travelling from Whanganui to Taupō, and today visitors still unwind at the nearby Tokaanu Thermal Pools after a day of adventures. Choose from the large public pool, shallow kids' pool or private family-sized pools.

TOKAANU WHARF

History buffs will enjoy the nearby 260-metre-long slice of transportation history at Tokaanu Wharf. The wharf harks back to the late 1800s and operated well into the 1920s, when steamers chugged across Lake Taupō before improved road networks. It is one of the country's oldest wharf structures. Many voyagers travelling north stayed overnight to enjoy the soothing waters nearby before continuing their journey. Today, the restored wharf is a picturesque location to dangle a fishing line beside the calm shoreline.

KIKO LOOP TRACK |SH1 TŪRANGI|

SH1 TŪRANGI

KIKO LOOP TRACK

Nestled near the base of Kaimanawa Forest Park, a rugged forest with magical, moss-draped trees and a rousing chorus of native birds provides an adventure of two halves.

INFORMATION

GRADE: Medium.

ACCESSIBILITY: Dirt paths, sometimes narrow and rooty.

TIME: Allow 1 hour to 90 min to walk the 3.9 km loop. Allow 1 hour for biking.

FACILITIES: Toilet at the car park.

LOCATION: Turn off SH1 onto Kiko Road about 10 km north of Tūrangi. Follow the well-graded gravel road for 17 km to the car park.

DOGS: No dogs.

The first half of this little-known trail passes through regenerating forest where red and silver beech trees were once ravaged. But slowly, spongy moss appears beside the track, and the forest becomes more dense, with virgin beech trees and hundreds of kahakaha/perching lily clambering for space in the crooks of branches. Toutouwai/North Island robin can often be spotted following visitors, hoping to sample critters disturbed by footsteps on the forest floor.

Youngsters can easily navigate the undulating loop as it dips in and out of small, fern-filled gullies and over bridges back to the car park. The aluminium bands on the trees help prevent possums from munching on a rare species of red mistletoe growing in the area. Bring the essentials, including a first aid kit and warm clothing, as this walk is relatively isolated.

BIKE RIDING

The trail is rated an easy (Grade 2) ride for bikers, although we'd suggest it's more intermediate (Grade 3) and wouldn't suit inexperienced riders due to some steep, narrow sections.

IDENTIFY NATIVE TREES

While out and about adventuring, how many of these native trees can you recognise?

1. KAURI

This magnificent towering tree is one of the world's longest-living trees – they can live for more than 2000 years! But their survival is at risk from the incurable kauri dieback disease. The world's tallest kauri is the 51-metre-high Tāne Māhuta 'Lord of the Forest' in Waipoua Forest, Northland. Kauri timber was used by Māori for boat building and carving. The gum was used as a fire-starter.

2. TĪ KŌUKA CABBAGE TREE

Early New Zealand settlers used the trunks of these trees as chimneys in their huts because they are remarkably fire-resistant. The tree was also planted on the boundaries of important locations. They can grow from 12 to 20 metres high and the long, narrow leaves (which can be used as kindling) can be up to 1 metre long.

3. KAHIKATEA

These trees existed during the Jurassic period. Flying dinosaurs probably swooped down and munched on their fleshy seeds! It's our tallest native tree (growing up to 60 metres high) and often pokes through the forest canopy. The tree is common near rivers and in swamp forests. Māori used soot from burning the heartwood to create pigment for tā moko/traditional tattooing.

4. RIMU

When mature, these conifers can soar to more than 50 metres high and live for 800 years. This non-flowering tree has long, draping needles that are prickly to touch, and brown bark with flaky strips. It produces seeds only every 5–6 years. It was commonly known as red pine, and was used by European settlers to build homes and furniture.

5. TŌTARA

Māori used stone tools to carve massive waka from tōtara trunks – often taking more than a year to complete them. The rot-resistant wood was used for many purposes by Europeans, including railway sleepers and fence posts. This slow-growing tree reaches about 20 to 25 metres high. The largest known living tōtara, the Pouākani Tree, grows near Pureora in the central North Island.

6. PŪRIRI

These trees are an important food source for kererū/New Zealand pigeon, which also spread the tree's seeds. It is home to the caterpillar of New Zealand's largest moth, the pūriri moth, which drills a tunnel into the trunk. The average wingspan of the female moth is 15 centimetres. During pre-European times, Māori used the wood to make weapons and implements. The tree can grow to about 20 metres.

SH1 DESERT ROAD

URCHIN CAMPING AREA

Detour off SH1 to this free campsite within Kaimanawa Forest Park, surrounded by family-friendly walks and bike rides. For a night under the stars, bring a tent and enjoy the bright, clear skies. From Tūrangi, drive 15 kilometres south on SH1 before turning left on to Kaimanawa Road. A signposted turnoff is 3.5 kilometres further along the well-graded gravel road. The area is also the trailhead for mountain bike trails and Mount Urchin, an advanced 3- to 4-hour hike. For more information and maps, visit doc.govt.nz.

KAIMANAWA FOREST LOOP WALK

Kids will enjoy this easy loop through a forest dominated by red beech. Allow enough time to poke around in the upturned roots of toppled trees covered in fungi and look for forest critters.

Plenty of chirping from the treetops will entertain budding bird-spotters. This mini adventure isn't tiring, so it's ideal for even the youngest explorers.

INFORMATION: Well-graded dirt trail. Allow 20 min for the 1 km loop. Walking only. Toilet at the campsite. No dogs.

LOCATION: The loop starts and finishes near the campsite entrance.

URCHIN CAMPSITE TO PILLARS OF HERCULES

Wander through kāmahi and beech forest beside the Tongariro River on a leisurely out-and-back walk that includes a 40-metre-long suspension bridge over the deep Pillars of Hercules gorge. The fern-lined path is dual-use, so keep an ear out for mountain bikers.

The suspension bridge itself is a short, fun trip if a longer walk doesn't appeal. Look for the side road at the campsite junction that leads directly to the bridge.

INFORMATION: Well-graded dirt trail with steps. Allow 30 min (1.5 km) one way. Walking and biking only. Toilet at the campsite. No dogs.

LOCATION: Start from either the campsite or beside the suspension bridge.

PILLARS OF HERCULES GORGE

Churning through a narrow chasm, the Tongariro River leaves behind strange, twisted rock formations eroded from ancient lava. More than 350,000 years ago, when the lava cooled, it formed a solid base of andesite and ignimbrite rock which the river travels over. Luckily, the intriguing geology formation is easily visible by peering over the side of a bridge. If everyone is getting cabin fever on the drive, this makes an excellent quick side-trip off the Desert Road.

INFORMATION: Allow 5 to 10 min. Although there is limited traffic, take care while standing on the road bridge. No toilets.

LOCATION: 15 km south of Tūrangi, turn off SH1 onto Kaimanawa Road. The bridge is a further 2 km along.

LAKE ROTOPOUNAMU | SH47

SH47

LAKE ROTOPOUNAMU

Bring the togs and snacks to laze away an afternoon on the shoreline of this pounamu-coloured lake nestled in an ancient crater on Pīhanga.

INFORMATION

GRADE: Medium.

ACCESSIBILITY: Dirt paths with steps.

TIME: Allow 2 hours (6 km) for the loop.

FACILITIES: Toilet at Long Beach (BYO toilet paper).

LOCATION: From Tūrangi, drive towards National Park on SH47. Parking is available on the southern side of Te Ponanga Saddle (11 km from Tūrangi). Well signposted.

DOGS: No dogs.

According to Māori legend, the love-struck mountains Tongariro, Taranaki, Tauhara and Pūtauaki (Mount Edgecumbe) battled to win beautiful Pīhanga's affection, with the nearby Tongariro winning. Today, the battlefield surrounding the 1326-metre-high mountain is far less fiery, and Pīhanga has become a haven for native birds due to ongoing volunteer efforts. Listen out for the occasional kererū crash-landing in the canopy and the cheeky toutouwai/North Island robin.

The trail climbs steadily to the lake before settling into a leisurely stroll around its shoreline, which is lined with translucent kidney ferns. Long Beach sweeps around the far side of the lake and is ideal for picnicking and swimming.

Then, heading home, pass under gnarly trees overhanging the trail and look for critters in the fallen logs before descending back to the car park.

SHORTER OPTION

For a shorter adventure that can be wrapped up within 1 hour, visit Five Minute Beach or Ten Minute Beach.

IMPORTANT

Take care when crossing the very busy road on a blind corner.

TŪRANGI
TONGARIRO RIVER LOOP TRACK

The rambling Tongariro River provides the backdrop for an easy loop which crams in plenty of highlights near Tūrangi, including a must-do scenic lookout.

Buggies and bikes are welcome on the loop, although some decent arm-strength is required while pushing kids up the grunty lookout path. But the views are worth it, with Pīhanga sitting prettily on the horizon and plenty of anglers to watch as they try their luck in the crystal-clear waters below.

The loop is part of the longer but excellent 15-kilometre-long Tongariro River Trail (p161), which is best tackled by jumping in the saddle for a two-wheeled adventure.

INFORMATION: Well-graded dirt and gravel trail. Allow 1 hour to walk the loop. Dogs on leads.

LOCATION: An easy starting point is at Taupahi Reserve Park on Taupahi Road. Bike or walk south along the river path and cross the Major Jones Bridge before heading north.

MOTUOAPA
MOTUOAPA CLIFF LOOKOUT WALK

Walk to the top of the volcanic cliffs behind Motuoapa for panoramic views of Stump Bay, Lake Taupō and the vast Te Matapuna Wetlands. Only glimpses of the sprawling wetland wedged beside SH1 and Lake Taupō are visible while driving, but by taking a short walk to the lookout, the diverse wetland habitat, home to globally threatened species of birds, can be admired. An impressive volunteer effort by Project Tongariro is underway to protect the wetlands for future generations. Find out more: tongariro.org.nz.

During the weekends, watch a steady stream of fishing boats leaving Motuoapa's small marina and heading onto the sparkly waters of Lake Taupō.

INFORMATION: Allow 15 min return. Dirt path with steps. Walking only. Dogs on leads.

LOCATION: Tangitu Street, Motuoapa Village, approximately 10 km north of Tūrangi.

KAKAHI
KAKAHI GLOWWORM TUNNEL

On the other side of Lake Taupō, this 100-metre-long logging relic with almost vertical pumice walls has become home to a dazzling show of glowworms after dark. Overhanging mānuka creates a tunnel-like effect above the narrow road, initially dug for a proposed railway but now connecting Kakahi village and the Whakapapa River. Glowworm lights pierce the shrubbery, and their display is worthy of a detour when heading home from the mountains or road-tripping to southern adventures. Plenty of grassy areas beside the river are perfect for kids to run around or have a picnic.

INFORMATION: Well-graded gravel road is suitable for walking, buggies and bikes. Keep an eye out for cars. Dogs on leads.

LOCATION: About 20 min drive from Taumarunui or National Park on SH4. Turn off onto Waitea Branch Road and go through Kakahi village to Te Rena Road.

TŪRANGI

TONGARIRO RIVER TRAIL

Jump in the saddle for an adventure alongside the meandering Tongariro River near Tūrangi — keep an eye out for whio/blue ducks surfing the rapids.

INFORMATION

GRADE: Easy.

ACCESSIBILITY: Well-graded dirt paths, boardwalks and suspension bridges. It's buggy-friendly from Taupahi Reserve Park to Major Jones Bridge for a 30-min return outing.

TIME: Allow 1 to 2 hours biking (15 km) return or 2 to 3 hours walking.

LOCATION: A good starting point is at Taupahi Reserve Park, Tūrangi.

DOGS: Under control.

Fifteen kilometres of smooth trails weave through picturesque native forests and past sprawling farmland on a great mix of broad, flat trails and slightly narrower sections. After a few kilometres of easy riding south from Taupahi Reserve Park, there are some short sharp switchbacks leading to stands of spindly kānuka before a gentle descent to the Tongariro National Trout Centre.

Here, you can try your hand at fishing during the school holidays or feed rainbow trout year-round. Then continue along moss-lined trails, past valleys covered in dense bush and ferns, and zigzag across boardwalks towards the Red Hut Bridge. The return trail reaches vantage points high above the river with views across farmland to Mount Tauhara (p145) and travels beneath towering stands of pine trees to Major Jones Bridge. Make a quick detour onto the suspension bridge to watch any anglers trying their luck with some of the nation's most astute trout.

Continue north to the turnaround point at the SH1 bridge, after the

only challenging climb to the Lookout Track — but efforts are rewarded with stunning views of Mount Pīhanga and the southern shoreline of Lake Taupō. Finally, a quick playground stop at Taupahi Reserve Park should burn off the last of everyone's energy.

SHORTER OPTION

A shorter option taking 30 to 45 minutes that still crams in plenty of highlights starts at the reserve, crosses Major Jones Bridge and then loops north before returning.

SH4 ŌWHANGO

OHINETONGA LAGOON

Dangle toes off a boardwalk stretching across a sparkling lagoon with its rippling reflections of native trees.

INFORMATION

GRADE: Medium.

ACCESSIBILITY: Well-graded dirt paths with steps and boardwalks.

TIME: Allow 1 hour for the lagoon loop.

FACILITIES: Toilet at the car park.

LOCATION: Turn off SH4 at Ōwhango onto Omaki Road, then left onto Whakapapa Bush Road. Plenty of parking beside the Whakapapa River bridge.

DOGS: No dogs.

This magical trail begins on the fringes of Tongariro Forest Park, beside the Whakapapa River. Spend a few moments on the bridge admiring the river where the elusive, endangered whio/ blue duck can sometimes be seen cruising the fast-flowing rapids. From the car park, the undulating path passes a summer swimming hole — chilled by streams trickling down the slopes of Mount Ruapehu — to a tree platform with a huggable ancient tōtara.

But the main attraction is a stunning lagoon surrounded by native forest with dragonflies flitting across its surface. A wooden boardwalk traversing the lagoon allows feet-dangling opportunities above the clear water, home to busy aquatic critters. From here, the path continues for another 5 minutes before popping out onto Whakapapa Bush Road. Then it's a pleasant downhill walk of about 1 kilometre back to the car park. At the northern tip of the lagoon, a small forested trail provides views of the lagoon from another angle.

SHORTER OPTION

For a quick lagoon experience, skip the bush walk and find the small signposted trail entrance on the right while driving down Whakapapa Bush Road. A 5-minute stroll beneath giant trees leads to the lagoon.

ŌWHANGO

The former mill town flourished in the early 1900s when the Main Trunk Line opened. This ease of transportation allowed a large-scale timber industry to develop, and 11 mills were built to process wood. Luckily, despite insatiable demand for timber, the recreational and scenic qualities of the rich forest at Ohinetonga meant it remained untouched, and in 1921 it was formally recognised as a reserve.

SH48 TO WHAKAPAPA VILLAGE

TAWHAI FALLS

An idyllic waterfall that is ideal for wringing out the last moments of mountain adventuring before heading home.

It's a short 400-metre-long stroll through mountain toatoa and beech forest to a viewing platform above the Whakapapanui Stream as it tumbles off a lava flow. The 13-metre-high falls plunge into a deep pool that *Lord of the Rings* fans will recognise as Gollum's pool.

From here, continue to the steps leading down to a rock cluster that offers even better views of the waterfall — look for the 'troll'-shaped rocks beside the pool. Allow time for paddling, picnicking and re-enacting *LOTR* scenes on the small beach.

The well-graded gravel path suits all adventurers, and, although there are a few steps, there's nothing strenuous about this outing. It's a worthy stop when visiting Tongariro National Park.

Endangered whio/blue ducks have been spotted further upstream, so keep an eye out for these well-camouflaged native ducks, which live on fast-flowing rivers and streams.

INFORMATION

GRADE: Easy.

ACCESSIBILITY: Well-graded gravel path with steps.

TIME: Allow 20 min (800 m) return, more for paddling and picnics.

LOCATION: 4 km before Whakapapa Village on SH48.

DOGS: No dogs.

MOUNDS WALK

A little further north on SH48 is the Mounds Walk. Wind past strange hummocky mounds to a vantage point to eyeball the perplexing landscape. Were the humps created during an ice age, or are they formed from debris from volcanic eruptions? Read the signs to find out! The short, easy walk is ideal for mountain views on a nice clear day. The road to Whakapapa Village goes straight through the middle of one mound, so take a peek at what lies inside. Allow 20 minutes return. Walking only. No dogs.

WHAKAPAPA VILLAGE

TARANAKI FALLS

Traverse a volcanic landscape and glimpse how mighty forces beneath the Central Plateau have shaped this UNESCO World Heritage site, before visiting a snow-fed waterfall plunging off a lava flow.

From Whakapapa Village, the undulating trail traverses the red tussock-covered flanks of Mount Ruapehu towards the 20-metre-high falls. Steps sidle down to a vantage point where the falls can be seen plummeting off a large andesite lava flow that erupted from Mount Ruapehu about 15,000 years ago. Rest up and enjoy the view before continuing downstream to the lower bridge, where the cascading Wairere Stream has eroded chasms into the rock. Finally, the trail disappears into mountain beech forest as it loops back to Whakapapa Village. Keep watch for some of the nation's smallest native birds — the pōpokotea/whitehead, riroriro/grey warbler and titipounamu/rifleman — in the treetops.

IMPORTANT

Stay hydrated and protected from the sun along the exposed upper trail during summer. The more sheltered lower track is a better out-and-back option on hot days and in dismal weather. Parking is available opposite the visitor centre or beside the golf course on SH48.

TONGARIRO NATIONAL PARK

Gifted to the nation by Māori chief Te Heuheu Tūkino IV in 1887, Tongariro National Park was the first national park recognised in New Zealand. It also holds dual UNESCO World Heritage status, recognising the mountains as spiritual and cultural entities.

The almost 80,000-hectare park is rife with volcanoes, and taking pride of place is Mount Doom. Even without fancy *Lord of the Rings* special effects, the 2291-metre-high volcanic cone Mount Ngāuruhoe broods, despite not having blown its top since 1975. For the energetic, New Zealand's best one-day walk, the Tongariro Alpine Crossing (p166), winds around its flanks en route to Mount Tongariro summit.

The trailhead for family-friendly adventures on the northern side of Mount Ruapehu is the small alpine village of Whakapapa. Don't miss exploring the visitor centre with its excellent skiing history and volcanic educational displays.

INFORMATION

GRADE: Medium.

ACCESSIBILITY: Well-graded gravel trail with steps and boardwalks.

TIME: Allow 2 hours (6 km) for the loop.

FACILITIES: Toilets at Whakapapa Village.

LOCATION: The trailhead is at the end of Ngāuruhoe Terrace, Whakapapa Village.

DOGS: No dogs.

WHAKAPAPA VILLAGE

WHAKAPAPA NATURE WALK

Navigate different alpine vegetation zones on a mini-adventure alongside a burbling snow-fed stream.

Looping beneath weather-beaten beech trees, this pint-sized adventure offers a short, accessible nature walk for all ages. Mossy banks line the buggy- and wheelchair-friendly concrete path leading to a small vantage point overlooking the Whakapapanui Stream. Signs along the way explain the different vegetation zones and which hardy plants thrive in sub-alpine environments.

This nature walk is a must-do when visiting Whakapapa Village, especially if the kids are averse to hiking longer trails. And, when completed, pop into the nearby motor camp store for ice creams or snacks.

For a longer adventure, follow the steps towards the river and look for kiwi prints on the sandy stream banks. A small picnic area near the car park allows loitering opportunities to enjoy the rugged alpine scenery. Visit during winter — but avoid snow clumps falling from the trees!

INFORMATION

GRADE: Easy.

ACCESSIBILITY: Flat concrete path. Optional steps.

TIME: Allow 15 min for the loop.

FACILITIES: Toilets opposite the motor camp and at the visitor centre.

LOCATION: Begins 250 metres past the visitor centre on the right. Small car park.

DOGS: No dogs.

TONGARIRO NATIONAL PARK

TONGARIRO ALPINE CROSSING

For the energetic, New Zealand's so-called best one-day walk climbs to the saddle between Mounts Ngāuruhoe and Tongariro before a final push to the Red Crater, then a steady descent past the sparking Emerald Lakes and into forest. At nearly 20 kilometres long, the Tongariro Crossing lets keen hikers traverse the country's oldest national park and gape at the dramatic high-altitude scenery.

INFORMATION: This is an alpine walk and requires hikers to prepare for all seasons in one day. For detailed information on the walk, visit doc.govt.nz. Walking only. No dogs.

SH48 BRUCE ROAD

IWIKAU VILLAGE

Don't miss jumping in the car for the 6-kilometre-long drive up to Iwikau Village at the base of the Whakapapa ski field on Mount Ruapehu. Summer or winter, this high vantage point surrounded by snow-fed streams trickling across the volcanic landscape is postcard-worthy. At the signposted Scoria Flats, there's plenty of roadside parking to stop and enjoy lunch on an active volcano. Yikes!

INFORMATION: Drive through Whakapapa Village on SH48 across Whakapapanui Stream to the car park at Iwikau Village. No dogs.

SILICA RAPIDS

Wander past tussock-covered lava flows and alpine bogs, with Mount Ruapehu providing an imposing backdrop. An easy trail visits the creamy-coloured Waikare Stream that bubbles to the surface at the base of a lava flow further up the valley.

INFORMATION: Allow 90 min return from Bruce Road (2.5 km from Whakapapa Village). Walking only. No dogs.

TAMA LAKES TRACK

If you have a spare 5 hours or so, the hike to Tama Lakes is stunning. Barren landscapes, mountain vistas and a steady ascent to two alpine lakes make the nearly 18 km return trail a popular option for families with older children.

INFORMATION: This is an alpine walk and requires hikers to prepare for all seasons in one day. For detailed information on the walk, visit doc.govt.nz. Walking only. No dogs.

RIDGE TRACK

A steady uphill trail through beech forest emerges above the treeline and continues past alpine shrubland to a viewing platform overlooking Whakapapa Village and Mount Ngāuruhoe. An excellent short outing to capture sunset over the volcanic landscape for folks loitering late in the village.

INFORMATION: Allow 40 min return. Walking only. Begins at the shelter opposite the motor camp. No dogs.

image © Paula Cooper

OHAKUNE MOUNTAIN ROAD

WAITONGA FALLS TRACK

Walk through mountain beech forest before emerging onto a sub-alpine landscape dimpled with bogs and grabbing a selfie at Tongariro National Park's tallest waterfall.

INFORMATION

GRADE: Medium.

ACCESSIBILITY: Well-graded gravel trail with steps and boardwalk.

TIME: Allow 80 to 100 min (4 km return) return.

FACILITIES: None.

LOCATION: The car park is 11 km up the Ohakune Mountain Road towards Tūroa Ski Area. Approximately 15 min drive from Ohakune Village.

DOGS: No dogs.

From the car park, the well-graded trail climbs steadily through sub-alpine mountain beech and kaikawaka/mountain cedar forest as it makes its way to the multi-tiered waterfall. At 39 metres tall, the falls are an excellent picnicking destination. And on a fine day the trail provides impressive views of Mount Ruapehu while navigating the boggy alpine zone.

Keep an eye out for the carnivorous sundews and bladderworts in the bog beside the boardwalk. To survive, these hungry plants trap and munch on little critters and single-celled microscopic animals. They thrive in soil that lacks nutrients, so the acidic bog is ideal. Often, the shallow pools have photo-worthy reflections of the mighty maunga.

The waterfall can be heard while navigating a final series of forested switchbacks before spying it plummeting into a rock-strewn valley. Keen explorers can reach the falls' base, but there is also a good perching spot to view the twisting falls and have a bite to eat near the forest edge.

The walk passes through alpine landscapes, so prepare for all seasons and pack warm clothes and wind- and waterproof jackets.

OHAKUNE MOUNTAIN ROAD

MANGAWHERO FALLS

Only minutes from the road, this waterfall offers impressive vistas with almost zero walking required. The 28-metre-high waterfall is worth visiting in all seasons. During warmer months, the falls plummet into a barren, rocky pool, while spectacular icicles can form around the waterfall in winter. A short walk through beech forest — stunted due to exposure to the harsh climate near the bushline — leads to a viewing platform.

INFORMATION: Walking only. 16 km up Ohakune Mountain Road. No dogs.

SH49 TOWARDS WAIŌURU

LAKE ROTOKURA WALK

Dry Lake is reached first, after strolling through picturesque native forest, but further along is Lake Rotokura, renowned for its healing waters. Surrounded by beech forest, the broad lake also reflects Mount Ruapehu on fine, still days. Because the lake is tapu, please do not fish or eat nearby. Wooden platforms beside Dry Lake can be used for picnicking.

INFORMATION: Walking only. Allow 30 min return. Add on another 30 min to walk around Lake Rotokura. 12 km from Ohakune on SH49 towards Waiōuru. Turn onto Karioi Station Road and drive for 1 km. No dogs.

THE BIG CARROT

It's hard to miss the enormous 7.5-metre-high carrot surrounded by a vegetable-themed adventure park on Ohakune's eastern fringes. Challenge the family on the obstacle course or let the kids loose on the slides, exercise equipment, nets and swings. It's one of the region's best playgrounds and has plenty of seating and picnic tables.

INFORMATION: Toilets. SH49, east Ohakune.

MANGAWHERO RIVER WALKWAY

A scenic riverside trail follows the snow-fed Mangawhero River, offering pleasant family strolling or easy bike riding. Then return the same way or wander through the streets of the laid-back mountain town at the base of Mount Ruapehu.

INFORMATION: Allow 60 to 100 min return. Old Station Road or Ayr Street, Ohakune.

image © Visit Ruapehu

OHAKUNE MOUNTAIN ROAD

For thrill-seeking bike riders, a 1000-metre-long freewheeling descent from Tūroa Ski Area at 1700 metres above sea level provides jaw-dropping views of dramatic volcanic landscapes and sub-alpine forest zooming past. It's also doable by car if energy levels are low.

INFORMATION: Allow 1 hour (17 km). Bike shuttles available to Tūroa Ski Area.

image © Visit Ruapehu

OHAKUNE MOUNTAIN ROAD

MANGAWHERO FOREST WALK

Cross the bridge and embark on a leisurely one-hour loop alongside the Mangawhero River at the feet of Mount Ruapehu.

The undulating trail heads upstream beside the chilly stream, providing toe-dipping and rock-hopping opportunities for hardy folks. Immediately after walking through a cut log, the track crosses a large volcanic crater. Although it's not very visible, it's still worth stopping and looking for subtle undulations in the landscape.

Interesting features along the way will keep kids engaged: a bridge across a picturesque forest stream for a friendly game of Poohsticks, a low rock cave for critter hunting and a dense native forest to test the skills of budding botanists.

At its highest point, the walk crosses the Ohakune Mountain Road before heading back to the car park through giant rimu, mataī and kahikatea, which can reach more than 30 metres above the forest floor.

INFORMATION

GRADE: Medium.

ACCESSIBILITY: Well-graded dirt trail with some rooty sections.

TIME: Allow 1 hour (3 km return) for the loop.

FACILITIES: Toilets near the car park.

LOCATION: Plenty of parking at the base of Ohakune Mountain Road.

DOGS: No dogs.

RIMU WALK

Short on time? Grab a quick dose of nature on a leisurely 15-minute stroll that handily also suits buggies.

Beginning beside the Mangawhero Forest Walk trailhead, the trail veers to the left after the bridge before completing a loop back to the car park. Without exerting much energy, visitors are immediately plunged into a dimly lit forest brimming with native flora and fauna. Great for an end-of-day outing to tucker out the kids. No dogs or bikes.

SH4 HOROPITO

OHAKUNE OLD COACH ROAD

Grab the bikes and discover a historic cobbled road lost beneath dense forest for almost a hundred years.

INFORMATION

GRADE: Grade 3 (intermediate).

ACCESSIBILITY: The trail is also suitable for tag-along bikes for youngsters still gaining confidence on two wheels.

TIME: Allow 2 to 4 hours biking or 4 hours walking one way.

FACILITIES: Toilets and picnic areas alongside the trail.

LOCATION: Start from either Horipito or Ohakune.

DOGS: No dogs allowed in Tongariro National Park.

This historic trail was a critical transportation link between Ohakune and Raurimu before the Hapuawhenua Viaduct connected the unfinished northern and southern sections of the North Island Main Trunk Line in 1908. Horse-drawn coaches traversed the rugged trail through often freezing conditions, ferrying goods and people. But when trains began chugging their way across the lower reaches of Mount Ruapehu, the route became obsolete until restoration efforts began in the early 2000s.

The trail is easily explored on two wheels as it disappears into the lush sub-alpine forest, across bone-jangling cobblestone remnants, through a spooky railway tunnel and, for the brave, a cycle across the 284-metre-long, 45-metre-high curved old Hapuawhenua Viaduct.

This adventure can be tackled in both directions, but getting a shuttle to the more popular northern trailhead at Horopito provides an excellent outing that ticks off some impressive

engineering feats and historical sights — and has an overall downhill profile.

Before entering Tongariro National Park, the trail starts near the classic car-wreckers museum at Horopito, aka Smash Palace. Then it's easy riding through areas of native grasses, flax and ferns before arriving at the impressively large curved Taonui Viaduct.

The trail drops below the viaduct and climbs through the native forest to the selfie-worthy

Hapuawhenua Viaduct. On the far side of the old viaduct are picnic tables and toilets.

On the descent towards Ohakune, don't miss the hand-dug tunnel and learn about the construction of this engineering feat. The final section is a long, grassy downhill track to Marshalls Road car park before easy pedalling along a flat, quiet rural road back to Ohakune.

Take a breather at the rest spots dotted along this unearthed historical gem, part of the Mountains to Sea cycle trail.

IMPORTANT

Suitable for mountain bikes only, as the trail crosses gravel, steep and narrow sections, and bumpy cobblestones. Bring a bike repair kit, food, hydration and warm clothing for this relatively isolated adventure.

NGĀ ARA TŪHONO

MOUNTAINS TO SEA CYCLE TRAIL

Begin pedalling from high on the volcanic slopes of Mount Ruapehu before embarking on a thrilling descent through dense alpine forest, across towering viaducts, past the abandoned Bridge to Nowhere, to end beside the untamed Tasman Sea near Whanganui. Connecting two national parks, Tongariro and Whanganui, this multi-trail adventure has family-friendly options from a few hours to more adventurous multi-day outings. More trails are listed on their website.

FIND OUT MORE
mountainstosea.nz

FISHERS TRACK

An easy half-day ride through rural countryside with views of volcanic peaks, including the little-known Mount Hauhungatahi, at the southern end of the Taupō Volcanic Zone. Grade 2 (Easy), 2 to 3 hours return (27 km). Begins at National Park Village.

MANGAPURUA TRACK BRIDGE TO NOWHERE

Journey through a remote, long-deserted valley to the mystical Whanganui River and the Bridge to Nowhere. Choose to return by jet boat or bike back the same way. Grade 3 (Intermediate), 4 to 7 hours biking return (36 km). Multiple entry points. Visit the website for more details.

MARTON SASH AND DOOR TRAMWAY

An enjoyable short ride for most ages and abilities. A historic loop follows a bush tramway dating back to the early logging days. Grade 3 (Intermediate), 2 hours (18 km). Begins at National Park Village.

PUREORA FOREST PARK

FOREST TOWER TRACK

Clamber up a 12-metre-high tower for a bird's-eye view of a vast forest saved by eco-warriors.

INFORMATION

GRADE: Easy.

ACCESSIBILITY: Well-graded dirt trail and narrow wooden ladder.

TIME: Allow 30 min return.

FACILITIES: None.

LOCATION: From Barryville Road off SH30 southwest of Mangakino, take Pikiariki Road, then Bismarck Road.

DOGS: No dogs.

When conservationists climbed into the treetops of Pureora Forest Park 45 years ago, they saved an ancient rainforest from the ravages of logging. Protestors wedged makeshift platforms into weathered trees perched high above the forest floor. It was 1978, and logging within the rugged forest was rampant. At risk were vast stands of ancient forest. The protestors' sit-in was successful, and the area was recognised as a protected park later that same year. The trail passes near the protest site, where activists also hid beneath logs on the forest floor to stop logging operations.

Walk to the tower and enjoy the lush preserved forest and native ferns, spending time reading the signs about the plucky protestors. At the final corner, the wooden tower looms ahead. Eavesdrop on the haunting call of the kōkako, which has a growing population here, while climbing the narrow ladder.

For explorers jittery about heights, it's still worth walking to the tower's base to learn about the

area's fascinating conservation history.

D7 BULLDOZER

A historic logging relic beside the road is ideal for grabbing a quick 'dozer selfie while driving to the tower. This type of machinery was commonplace in the 1950s, with its winch even allowing the bulldozer to be lowered into tricky spots. With additional blades, these machines were versatile and allowed for quick log extraction.

PUREORA FOREST PARK

TŌTARA WALK

A remarkable forest remnant filled with giant tōtara, rimu and kahikatea provides shade on a short, accessible loop — an easy must-do adventure when visiting the park.

INFORMATION

GRADE: Easy.

ACCESSIBILITY: Well-graded dirt trail with boardwalks.

TIME: Allow 30 min (about 1 km) for the loop.

FACILITIES: Toilets near the car park.

LOCATION: Barryville Road, near the Timber Trail entrance, Pureora Forest Park.

DOGS: No dogs.

Peer up at majestic, mature trees from the wide, undulating trail as it loops through a dense forest remnant. Among the native trees and ferns, look for native birds such as tūī, miromiro/tomtits or kākā fluttering through the treetops. Don't miss the interactive bird-calling station with its various squawking sounds. Signs beside the trail identify native plants that might be unfamiliar. The nearby Pouākani tōtara (p174) is estimated to be 1800 years old. (It's unlikely any older trees survived the dense ash fallout that smothered the landscape from the Taupō Volcano eruption at that time.)

Visiting near dusk? Rug up warm and go hunting for glowworms on the damp, overhanging banks. Beside the trail are hundreds of bright-bummed gnats busily snaring dinner in their sticky, dangling lines. Find out more about these misnamed critters on page 66.

The well-signposted entrance is also the start of the 85-kilometre-long Timber Trail, one of New Zealand's Great Rides (p175).

NGAHERENGA CAMPSITE

Come armed with all the essentials to set up camp beside the picnic tables and fire pits at a campsite on the edge of Pureora Forest Park. Pack wood and fire-starters to start toasting marshmallows under the stars, to the accompaniment of squawking kākā.

The campsite is within easy strolling distance of the Tōtara Walk — perfect for a glowworm-hunting adventure at dusk.

INFORMATION

Bookings are required for the 16 non-powered sites suitable for campervans, caravans and tents.

Limited mobile reception. Long-drop toilet. Water. Accessible from Barryville/Maraeroa Roads off SH30. No dogs.

FIND OUT MORE
doc.govt.nz

LINK ROAD

CENTRE OF THE NORTH ISLAND

It hardly seems scientific, but a pin and a length of nylon helped discover the centre of the North Island. Deep within Pureora Forest Park, at the end of a short, picturesque walk surrounded by mossy trees, is an obelisk marking this prime location. By dangling a map of the North Island mounted onto cardboard bent to represent the Earth's curvature, registered surveyor John Wheeler found the map's centre of gravity in 1961, which indicated this isolated spot. However, Horahora and Waharoa have also been considered strong contenders for the geographical oddity. Peer into the trees on the northern side of the car park to see where the unmarked boardwalk begins.

INFORMATION: Well-graded dirt trail and boardwalks. Walking only. Wrap up warm in winter as the forest gets very chilly. No dogs.

LOCATION: Follow the signposted road off Link Road (accessible from either side of Pureora Forest Park) for 2.5 km, then left onto another gravel road leading to the car park.

SH30

POUĀKANI TŌTARA

This forest giant is the largest tōtara ever recorded and is seriously 'crick in the neck' high at nearly 35 metres. Even the crown of the magnificent native is hard to spot through its gnarly branches laden with epiphytes. But despite its hidden upper reaches, the impressively girthy tree is worth visiting.

The trail is undulating and can be rooty underfoot in places, and an occasional windfall tree may need to be navigated around. In winter, the track can become soggy, so bring a spare pair of sneakers or, even better, gumboots.

Walk around the bedraggled fence crushed by plummeting epiphytes surrounding the main attraction to admire the tree from all angles. It's remarkable that the tree — which could be nearly 1800 years old and has a whopping girth of 12 metres — escaped being logged for its prized timber.

INFORMATION: Dirt trail, sometimes rooty. Walking only. Allow 40 min to 1 hour return. No dogs.

LOCATION: On SH30, 10 min east of Pureora Field Base, Barryville Road.

PLAINS ROAD

BURIED FOREST

Smothered in ash following the most recent Taupō volcanic eruption some 1800 years ago, a small section of the flattened forest was accidentally uncovered by a digger driver in 1983. Unfortunately, only a few fallen trunks are visible in the swampy overgrown landscape, so a healthy imagination is required to visualise the immense force of the eruption which devastated the area.

At the end of Plains Road, follow the sound of the small stream northwest — not the main river. Unfortunately, the trail is no longer maintained, so it could take a couple of minutes scrambling through the shrubbery, but fun nonetheless. Peer into the small stream to see a handful of black logs almost hidden beneath the overhanging banks.

INFORMATION: Rough, unformed trail. Allow 10 min return. Walking only. No facilities. No dogs.

LOCATION: About 10 min down Plains Road off Barryville Road. Take care on the narrow road as it can be boggy after heavy rain. 4WD vehicles are recommended.

PUREORA FOREST PARK

BIKING THE TIMBER TRAIL

The Timber Trail is one of New Zealand's Great Rides and takes riders on a journey past unique heritage sites, deep gorges and epic views of the central North Island. The 85-kilometre-long trail through Pureora Forest Park opened in 2013 after two old forest logging tramways were unearthed from dense vegetation to form a single route. Thousands of hours of bush-bashing and trail-building have resulted in 35 standard bridges and 8 impressive suspension bridges spanning the mountainous countryside. For trail information, maps and accommodation options, visit timbertrail.nz.

PUREORA FOREST PARK

TIMBER TRAIL

The entire trail can be biked in two sections, each taking between 5 and 7 hours to complete, with many bikers choosing to camp at Piropiro, about halfway at 40 kilometres, or stay at the nearby lodge.

The trail has a predominantly wide and smooth surface, with the occasional decent climb and trickier section. It's suitable for reasonably fit riders with a tool kit and basic mechanical skills due to its remoteness. Highlights along the way include suspension bridges, virgin rainforest and summitting the highest point at 971 metres above sea level before winding past pioneering remnants and the historic Ōngarue Spiral before completing the adventure.

INFORMATION: 85 km. A mix of Grade 2 (easy) and Grade 3 (intermediate) trails. No dogs.

PUREORA FOREST PARK

PUREORA CRAWLER TRACTOR LOOP

A quick bike ride — or longer stroll — delves deep into native forest filled with birdlife to an abandoned 2-tonne Caterpillar Crawler tractor and 'konaki' sled, relics from the region's logging days.

Start from the same trailhead as the Timber Trail, and bike about 3 kilometres before detouring onto the tractor trail. Bring snacks and relax on the wooden benches, admiring the stranded tractor used during the 1930–40s.

Then continue to the gravel Link Road, which returns to the car park. Or return the same way.

INFORMATION: Allow 1 hour (7 km) return biking or 90 min walking. Start from Barryville Road, Pureora Forest Park. No dogs. Toilet at the car park.

ŌNGARUE

ŌNGARUE TO THE SPIRAL

The only rideable spiral in the world is the reward for a steady 8 kilometres of uphill pedalling from Ōngarue.

It's an impressive sight. Most New Zealand tram routes have been destroyed, so seeing this with its lower-level bridge, a deep cutting, curved tunnel, and the complete circle of track and over-bridge is worth the uphill slog.

Although this section of the trail isn't as bush-clad as the first 70 kilometres of the Timber Trail, the smooth coasting back to the car park on pumice tracks is good fun.

INFORMATION: Allow 3 to 4 hours (16 km) return. No dogs. Start from the Bennett Road car park off Ngākonui–Ōngarue Road, Ōngarue.

All images © Timber Trail

LINK ROAD

MOUNT PUREORA

Take the shortest route to the top of Mount Pureora for views across the Central Plateau and towards the rugged west coast.

Save this adventure for a fine day to see the peaks of Mounts Taranaki and Ruapehu and views across Lake Taupō and the Kaimanawa Ranges on arrival at the summit. An impressive vista for only one hike!

Starting from about 800 metres above sea level, the well-maintained trail delivers hikers to the 1165-metre-high summit relatively quickly, which means the high peak can be enjoyed without traversing too many foothills. A boardwalk leads to an exposed, shrubby summit above the forest line, where hikers can take a well-deserved break. Come prepared with warm clothes, as the summit gets chilly.

INFORMATION: Allow 2 hours (2.6 km) one way. Walking only. No dogs. No toilets.

LOCATION: Parking is available about 14 km along Link Road, off Barryville Road, Pureora Forest Park.

image © John Carman

SH32 WESTERN BAY ROAD

WAIHĀHĀ HUT

Follow the picturesque Waihāhā River as it winds through shrubland before entering a dense podocarp forest leading to a rustic, cosy, 10-bunk hut perched on a small clearing. Along the way, stop at plenty of vantage points to admire the diverse landscape.

It's the perfect backcountry trip for kids wanting a slightly more adventurous outing. Go old-school and spark some family rivalry while playing cards by candlelight.

It's also an intermediate (Grade 3) mountain bike trail (allow 2 to 3 hours one way) if hiking doesn't appeal.

INFORMATION: Purchase hut tickets from the Department of Conservation. Bookings are not required. Beds are on a first-come, first-served basis. Allow 3 hours (9.4 km one way) to reach the hut. No dogs.

LOCATION: Off Western Bay Road (SH32).

SH32 WESTERN BAY ROAD

RIMU WALK

Climb through dense rimu forest to a vantage point with views of Mount Pureora's peak above the tops of mighty natives that survived the area's logging days. Beginning on the eastern side of Pureora Forest Park, the walk crosses the swift Kakaho Stream, passing tangled undergrowth of supplejack vines before a generous number of stairs ascend the boulder-strewn forest slope to the wooden lookout. See native trees poking through the forest canopy and listen for birdsong. To the west, glimpses of Mount Pureora are visible.

From the lookout, follow the path as it descends towards the exit point on Kakaho Road. Turn right to reach the campsite a couple of hundred metres further down the road.

INFORMATION: Allow 1 hour (about 1.7 km) for the loop. Walking only. No dogs.

LOCATION: Begins from Kakaho Campsite, about 5.5 km along Kakaho Road off Western Bay Road (SH32).

SH32 WESTERN BAY ROAD

WAIHORA LAGOON

Step back into primeval New Zealand to see a rare wetland lagoon surrounded by swamp forests and fragile plants.

INFORMATION

GRADE: Easy.

ACCESSIBILITY: Well-graded dirt trails and boardwalks. Sometimes boggy during winter. Suitable for outdoorsy buggies when dry.

TIME: 30 min return.

FACILITIES: None.

LOCATION: Waihora Road, off SH32. Follow the gravel road for approximately 7 km. The very rough road suits 4WD vehicles.

DOGS: No dogs.

A short stroll leads to a rare ephemeral wetland entirely fed by rainwater created by dense layers of ash from the Taupō volcanic eruption. During dry spells, the shallow lagoon can become a small–middling puddle, but after heavy rain the lagoon overflows into the surrounding swamp forest, which is dominated by towering rimu and kahikatea that create reflections in the dark water.

Despite the extremely clean and pure water, no fish live in the lagoon because of its fluctuating levels. However, swarms of tadpoles are often seen here before turning into golden bell frogs, an import from Australia.

Using the raised walkways saves the tiny, rare plants growing on the lagoon's edge. In the centre of the lagoon grow more fragile water-loving plants, such kutakuta/bamboo spike sedge.

KAHAKAHA
PERCHING LILY

These epiphytes nestle in the crooks of the trees where humus (soil formed by decomposing leaves and other plant material) has accumulated over time. Early European bushmen called them 'widowmakers' because they often fell from milled trees, and it was not life-extending to be under a massive specimen as it plummeted to the ground. The young plant has the classic fan shape and often grows in large colonies in tree branches. They are also known as tank lilies.

Te Papa Atawhai | Department of Conservation
Te Taura Whiri i te Reo Māori | Māori Language Commission
Te Tāhuhu o te Mātauranga | Ministry of Education

Kia Kaha te Reo Taiao

Language of the Environment
Give it a Go!

Oropuare | Vowels

There are five vowel sounds in Māori. They can be pronounced 'short' or 'long'. The long vowel is marked with a macron.

a is close or similar to f**a**ther

e is close or similar to dr**e**ss

i is close or similar to s**ee**

o is close or similar to th**ou**ght

u is close or similar to g**oo**se

a e i o u

ā ē ī ō ū

When the vowel is long, with a macron above it, say the vowel for twice as long.

Ororua | Two Vowels and Diphthongs

When two different vowels are together they either retain their basic sounds and are pronounced one after the other or they 'glide' from one vowel to the other vowel to make a different sound we call a diphthong.

Examples of common diphthongs are *ai, ae, au, ou, oe, ao.*

ai oe
ae au
ou ao

Orokati | Consonants

There are 10 consonants, they are:

h k m n ng
p r t w wh

ng as in si**ng**er

wh as in **f**ilm

r is usually not rolled. The **r** sound is created when the tip of the tongue briefly touches the top of the mouth behind the teeth.

Mai i ngā maunga ki te moana

Mountains to the sea

He aha ka kitea i te wai?

What can you see in the water?

tuna
eel

piharau, kanakana
lamprey

īnanga
whitebait

whio
blue duck

kōkopu
giant bully

mātāwainuku
underground aquifer

korio, tāheke
rapids

Me tūpato ki te rere o te wai

Be careful of the current

taniwha
guardian
protector

kapowai
dragonfly

kōtuku
white heron

repo
wetlands

kōhatu awa
river stone

wai māori
fresh water

kēwai
kōura wai māori
freshwater crayfish

Kaua e whakakino i te wai

Don't pollute the water

Kaua e taraiwa i runga i te kūkūpango
Don't drive on the riverbed

awa
river, stream

moana, roto
lake

Me kaukau tāua ki te awa

Let's meet at the river for a swim

hīrere, tāheke
waterfall

puna kaukau
swimming hole

Tiakina a Papatūānuku

Protect the Earth Mother

Me mātua whai i te ara

Stay on the track

Me hīkoi haere tāua i te puihi ā ngā rā whakatā?

Shall we go for a bushwalk this weekend?

He aha te rākau hei whakatō mā tāua?

What tree shall we plant?

Me mahara ki te whakapaipai i ō hū

Remember to clean your shoes

whenua land

ara track

ngahere forest

ponga silver fern

kōtukutuku fuchsia

nīkau palm tree

puihi bush

rau leaf

ongaonga stinging nettle

māra kai cultivation and vegetable garden

kōpurawhetū – werewere kōkako native fungi – blue mushroom

rongoā medicine

rautini Chatham Island Christmas tree

pōānanga native clematis

tātarāmoa bush lawyer vine

tawhai beech tree

pikopiko edible fern shoots

kōtaratara Māori holly

patupaiarehe fairy people

pūtu hīkoi tramping boots

āniwaniwa, uenuku rainbow

I kite au i te kōtuku i te rangi nei

I saw a kōtuku today

manu
bird

pīwakawaka
pīwaiwaka
tīrairaka
fantail

ruru
morepork

kāhu
hawk

pīpīwharauroa
shining cuckoo

tīeke
saddleback

mohua
yellowhead

Waimarie katoa tātou ki te kite i te tini o ngā kererū i konei

We are so lucky to see so many kererū here

Aue! Whakarongo ki te kōkī hāpara

Wow! Listen to the dawn chorus

pepeke ngārara
insect

tuatara
reptile

mokomoko
lizard

He pūkeko tērā, he takahē rānei?

Is that a pūkeko or a takahē?

wētā punga
giant wētā

ngata
giant snail

pekapeka
bat

pepeketua
Archey's frog

pepetuna
pūriri moth

ngaro huruhuru
native bee

WAIKATO 9

NORTH WAIKATO 10

HAKARIMATA RANGE 21

HAMILTON 24

TE AWA RIVER RIDE 38

WAIPĀ 40

PIRONGIA FOREST PARK 50

WEST WAIKATO 54

RAGLAN 57

WAITOMO 66

HAURAKI RAIL TRAIL 70

EAST WAIKATO 73

TE AROHA 74

KARANGAHAKE GORGE 82

SOUTH WAIKATO 85

WAIKATO RIVER TRAILS 86

BAY OF PLENTY 91

WAIHI & WAIHI BEACH 92

KATIKATI 96

TAURANGA 99